ARMED CONFLICT IN LEBANON, 1982: HUMANITARIAN LAW IN A REAL WORLD SETTING

by

Sally V. Mallison

and

W. Thomas Mallison

Published by the American Educational Trust

Bodies of Lebanese killed during Israeli aerial attacks on Beirut during the first week of the June, 1982 invasion lie amidst the rubble of bombed buildings (above). Relatives of victims trapped under rubble from an Israeli air raid on Aug. 7 watch tensely as rescuers pick through the debris of a destroyed residential apartment building in Beirut.

ARMED CONFLICT IN LEBANON, 1982: HUMANITARIAN LAW IN A REAL WORLD SETTING

Contents

Foreward to The Second Edition

This book is a reflection of the Mallisons' long-standing professional concern with the protection of victims of armed conflict through the international humanitarian law. They consider the basic legal distinction between aggression and self-defense of primary importance in maintaining the world legal order and protecting elementary human values. Until the central objective of eliminating international armed conflict is achieved, they believe that it is vital to mitigate its horrors by applying the relevant law.

The first, 1983, edition of this book applied the humanitarian law to the grim events of the Israeli attack-invasion of June, 1982. The authors used both Israeli and Western sources in presenting the facts of the violations of law. They also relied upon on-the-spot reports of Lieutenant-General Callaghan of Ireland, the commander of the United Nations Interim Force in Lebanon (UNIFIL), in establishing the facts leading up to the June 1982 attack-invasion. In addition to the customary law of aggression and self-defense which is incorporated into article 51 of the United Nations Charter, the law that is applied includes the treaty law of Hague Convention IV of 1907 and of the Geneva Conventions for the Protection of War Victims of 1949.

In addition to the material previously presented, this second, 1985, edition contains an entirely new chapter (Chapter IV) concerning United States involvement in the attack-invasion. This is based on new material revealed in the 1984 book by former U.S. Secretary of State Alexander M. Haig, Jr. entitled, *Caveat: Realism, Reagan, and Foreign Policy,* which corroborates the facts presented by the Israeli investigative reporter, Mr. Zeev Schiff, in an article entitled "The Green Light" in the Spring, 1983 number of *Foreign Policy* magazine.

The first edition of this book, thoroughly documented like the new chapter, is already a standard reference for the application of international law to the 1982 conflict in Lebanon. With the introduction of new material drawn from Haig's writing, this second edition is also a sad reminder to Americans of their own government's abandonment in the Middle East of its traditional role in the world as protector of human rights, impartial arbiter among contending nations, and upholder of international law.

Andrew I. Killgore
President, American
Educational Trust,
and Retired U.S. Ambassador

1

Preface

The maintenance of public order is the most basic task of any legal system, whether domestic or international. The responsibility of a domestic order system is to exercise effective community control over private violence. In the same way, the responsibility of a world legal order is to exercise effective community control of international violence and coercion. The authors believe that if a minimum order system is to be achieved in the world community, it must be based on the customary and treaty law which states have developed through the centuries to protect human and material values. Without such a minimum order, the world will quickly degenerate into the situation where the law of the jungle—might makes right—prevails. In the era of weapons of mass destruction, this could mean the end of world civilization as we know it.

Much has been published about the factual situation of the Israeli attack on the Palestinian people and invasion of Lebanon in the summer of 1982. However, very little attention has been paid to the relevant principles of international law. The authors have attempted in this study to set forth the applicable law and to apply it to the fact situation. If the law is to be applied and its violation to be considered, a detailed compilation of the relevant specific facts is necessary. Although these may appear unpleasantly graphic, the authors have in all cases endeavoured to use only sources, newspaper and other, which are considered to be the most accurate and reliable available. In this respect, the authors have been gratified to note that reliable Israeli sources buttress the basic facts reported by the media in Great Britain and the United States.

It is the authors' conviction that unless there is a return to the rule of law in the Middle East, the violence will be accelerated, and the probable alternative to the achievement of at least a minimum legal order will be a further destructive war in the area with the possibility of a world conflagration of mutual mass destruction. It is imperative that the community of states take action based on law in order to effect peace with justice in Palestine and remove the present threat to the world peace and security.

The authors wish to express particular thanks to the staff of the American Educational Trust for the care which they have given to the production of this book, and to the many friends who have encouraged and assisted in this work. Special appreciation goes to Mr. John Reddaway for his valuable suggestions and to Ms. Nancy Jo Nelson and Mr. George W. Lindley, Jr. for efficient research assistance.

I. The Factual Situation

A. The Background: The Lebanese Internal Conflict

A comprehensive examination of the relevant background is beyond the scope of the present inquiry. It is necessary, however, to mention some of its aspects. Entirely apart from the problem of the displaced Palestinians who have taken refuge there, Lebanon has basic internal causes of strife resulting from socio-economic tension, intra-elite authority conflict, sectarian hostility, and the clash of identities and priorities.[1] This has resulted in a persistent authority problem as the various groups struggle for domination.

Particularly since 1967, Lebanon has been a natural, although sometimes somewhat reluctant, sanctuary for Palestinians who have fled or been driven from their homes in what is today Israel, the West Bank, and Gaza.[2] It has also been the location of the Palestine Liberation Organization (PLO) political leadership and infrastructure. The latter includes both military and civilian components. Its civilian structure places emphasis upon schools (predominately at the elementary level), other academic and research activities, and medical facilities, although there are some handicraft, manufacturing, and financial operations.[3]

This Palestinian functional state-within-a-state was a further divisive factor in a Lebanon where the traditional pluralist order was already unravelling in the face of regional as well as internal pressures. Initial support given the Palestinians by many Lebanese reflected a common commitment to the Arab cause and the cultural perception of the Palestinians as brothers.[4] Inevitably, however, the long-term presence and increasing organization of the Palestinian community, and the accompanying and virtually routine Israeli military assaults on south Lebanon and Beirut which the Palestinian presence occasioned, led to a split in the ranks of Lebanese tolerance. In particular, the right-wing, largely Christian factions whose dominant political and economic status depended upon the maintenance of the mechanistically apportioned confessional system of government, became hostile to the threatening presence of the largely Muslim Palestinian refugee population. The presence of the organized Palestinian military forces added to the friction.[5]

---

1. Hudson, "The Palestinian Factor in the Lebanese Civil War," 32 *Mid. E. J.* 270 (1978).
2. Cooley, "The Palestinians" in *Lebanon in Crisis* at 21-29 (Haley and Snider, eds., 1979).
3. Wall Street J., Oct. 22, 1979, p. 1, col. 1, cont. p. 21, cols. 1-3.
4. *Supra* note 1 at 264.
5. *Id.* at 267.

Serious confrontation between the right-wing dominated Lebanese government and army and the Palestinians began in 1969 and led to the renowned Cairo Agreement of that year which attempted to regulate the armed Palestinian presence and reconcile it with Lebanese sovereignty.[6] The agreement was amended in 1970 and affirmed in 1973 following renewed Lebanese-Palestinian violence.[7]

The inevitable collapse of order occurred in 1975 with the outbreak of the Civil War. Palestinians, allied with largely Muslim, leftist Lebanese forces seeking reforms in the Lebanese political system, confronted right-wing Lebanese forces seeking to maintain their political and economic dominance. Thousands of civilian casualties resulted, the Lebanese economy was wrecked, and the constitutional system created at the termination of the French Mandate was in shambles.[8] Fearing a leftist victory in the spring of 1976, substantial units of the Syrian Army began moving into Lebanon in April with the stated objective of stopping, or at least reducing, the internal conflict.[9] In a move to stem divisions in Arab ranks over the Syrian military intervention, the Arab League met in emergency session in Cairo on June 9th, called for a cease-fire, and agreed to establish a token Arab peacekeeping force to be sent to Lebanon.[10] Large scale fighting continued, however, until October 18 when representatives of Saudi Arabia, Kuwait, Syria, Lebanon, Egypt and the PLO met in Riyadh and agreed to a cease-fire and an expanded 30,000 man Arab peacekeeping force.[11] Interpreted in Beirut as an Arab mandate for continued Syrian political and military intervention in Lebanon,[12] the Riyadh accord was affirmed by 19 of 21 representatives of Arab nations and the PLO at a meeting of the Arab League in Cairo on October 25.[13] The enlarged peacekeeping force was to consist mainly of Syrian troops already in place and was to be financed by the Arab League.[14] It was specified that it would act under the overall command of President Sarkis of Lebanon.[15] Since that time the mandate has been renewed periodically at the request of the Lebanese government and the forces continued to operate under the multilateral authority of the League of Arab States until the mandate expired July 27, 1982 during the Israeli seige of Beirut.[16]

B. The International Conflict and the July 24, 1981 Cease-Fire

There has also been a continuing international conflict situation in southern Lebanon for many years before the intense hostilities of June, 1982. Professor Michael Hudson has described a part of it in these terms:

[T]he PLO was unable to eliminate cross-border operations altogether, because rejectionist Palestinian groups were still operating independently. Israeli reprisals grew ever

---

6. *Supra* note 2 at 29-30.
7. *Id.* at 31-32.
8. See generally M. Deeb, *The Lebanese Civil War* (1980).
9. Syrian intervention was with "tacit approval" by the United States (New York Times, June 2, 1976, p. 1, col. 2), Israeli acquiescence (Wash. Star, April 11, 1976, p. 1, col. 6), and right-wing Lebanese support (New York Times, June 6, 1976, p. 1, col. 8).
10. New York Times, June 9, 1976, p. 14, col. 6.
11. *Id.* Oct. 19, 1976, p. 1, col. 6, cont. p. 3, cols. 1-2.
12. *Id.*, Oct. 20, 1976, p. 4, cols. 1-4 at col. 1.
13. *Id.*, Oct. 26, 1976, p. 11, cols. 1-6 at cols. 1-2.
14. *Id.*, Oct. 27, 1976, p. 1, col. 1, cont. p. 3, cols. 3-4 at p. 1, col. 1.
15. *Id.* at p. 3, col. 3.
16. Wash. Post, July 28, 1982, p. A16, cols. 3-4.

fiercer so that by mid-1974 much of life in south Lebanon was disrupted. For example, after the PFLP-GC [Popular Front for the Liberation of Palestine-General Command] attack on Maalot on May 15 Israeli air force squadrons attacked a number of Lebanese towns and Palestinian refugee camps killing at least 50 civilians and wounding 200. Altogether, in the 44 major Israeli attacks into Lebanon between mid-1968 and mid-1974, approximately 880 Lebanese and Palestinian civilians had been killed, according to Lebanese government sources.[17]

Israeli plans for an attack-invasion of Lebanon were made a considerable time before they were implemented. Among the early references to such an operation was the entry in the diary of Israel's first Prime Minister, David Ben Gurion, for May 21, 1948 where he wrote:

> The Achilles heel of the Arab coalition is the Lebanon. Muslim supremacy in this country is artificial and can easily be overthrown. A Christian State ought to be set up here, with its southern frontier on the river Litani. We would sign a treaty of alliance with this State....[18]

The *Personal Diary* of Mr. Moshe Sharett, when he was serving as Prime Minister as well as Foreign Minister of Israel, includes a letter from Mr. Ben Gurion dated February 27, 1954 which reads in part:

> It is clear that Lebanon is the weakest link in the Arab League.... The creation of a Christian State is therefore a natural act; it has historical roots and it will find support in wide circles in the Christian world, both Catholic and Protestant.... [N]ow is the time to bring about the creation of a Christian State in our neighborhood. Without our initiative and our vigorous aid this will not be done. It seems to me that this is the *central duty,* or at least one of the central duties, of our foreign policy.[19]

Mr. Sharett's *Diary* also records a meeting of senior officials on May 16, 1954 where Mr. Ben Gurion stated that the time was propitious for action concerning Lebanon because of tensions between Syria and Iraq as well as internal trouble in Syria. Major General Dayan, then the Chief of Staff, expressed enthusiastic support. In the words of Mr. Sharett:

> According to him [Dayan] the only thing that's necessary is to find an officer, even just a Major. We should either win his heart or buy him with money to make him agree to declare himself the savior of the Maronite population. Then the Israeli army will enter Lebanon, will occupy the necessary territory, and will create a Christian regime which will ally itself with Israel.[20]

The Ben Gurion-Dayan approach was not implemented at that time.

Although there were many relatively minor Israeli ground incursions into Lebanon (in addition to repeated aerial attacks) the first major invasion did not take place until 1978. The March 1978 Israeli invasion of southern Lebanon up to the Litani River was a "watershed" event. On March 11, 1978 11 Palestinians seized two buses filled with sightseers on the Tel Aviv-Haifa Road and attempted to drive to the city. A gun battle erupted at a road block and 36 Israelis and nine of the Palestinians were killed.[21] On March 14, in alleged retaliation for the incident, the Israelis attacked across the international border and continued north until they reached the Litani River. The ground operations were preceded by

---

17. *Supra* note 1 at 267.
18. Quoted in Bar Zohar, *The Armed Prophet* 139 (London, 1967).
19. Quoted in L. Rokach, *Israel's Sacred Terrorism: A Study Based on Moshe Sharett's Personal Diary and Other Documents* 25 (1980).
20. *Id.* at 28.
21. Wash. Post, Mar. 15, 1978, p. A1, cols. 1-6 at col. 3.

heavy aerial and artillery bombardments which resulted in substantial civilian casualties.[22] Israeli Defense Minister Weizmann stated on March 15:

> This is an operation attempting to—and I think it will succeed—destroy and liquidate as best as possible concentrations of terrorists in southern Lebanon.[23]

The Security Council of the United Nations acted on the matter on March 19, 1978 by adopting resolution 425.[24] The first two operative paragraphs called for respect for Lebanese territorial integrity, and Israeli cessation of military action and withdrawal "forthwith" of its armed forces from Lebanon. The third operative paragraph established what was subsequently termed the United Nations Interim Force in Lebanon (UNIFIL) in these words:

> *Decides,* in the light of the request of the Government of Lebanon, to establish immediately under its authority a United Nations interim force for Southern Lebanon for the purpose of confirming the withdrawal of Israeli forces, restoring international peace and security and assisting the Government of Lebanon in ensuring the return of its effective authority in the area, the force to be composed of personnel drawn from Member States.

Before Israeli armed forces withdrew from Lebanon on June 13, 1978 they established a zone across southern Lebanon, and the first stage of the Ben Gurion plan for Lebanon recorded in Mr. Sharett's *Personal Diary* was put into operation almost three decades later.[25] The zone was placed under the authority of a renegade Lebanese military faction headed by Saad Haddad, formerly a major in the Lebanese Army. Thereafter, Major Haddad's forces were supplied, paid, and controlled by the Government of Israel.[26] UNIFIL subsequently was established in a zone to the north and west of the Haddad forces (termed the *de facto* forces by UNIFIL), but has not been able to carry out its functions in the zone controlled by the Government of Israel through Major Haddad.[27]

On June 17, 1981 the Government of Israel conducted a massive aerial bombing of Beirut which caused 300 civilian deaths and a much larger number of

---

22. According to the U.S. Congressional Research Service, by March 22, 1978 approximately 700 Lebanese and Palestinian civilians had been killed and more than 250,000 were made homeless. *Palestine and the Palestinians* 29 (Issue Brief No. IB76048, Oct. 23, 1979).
23. Press conference, *The Search for Peace in the Middle East: Documents and Statements, 1967-1979,* 340 (U.S. Congressional Research Service, 1979).
24. *22 U.N. SCOR* at 5, Doc. S/INS/34 (1978).
25. *Supra* note 20.
26. *The Middle East* 178 (Cong. Quarterly Inc., 5th Edition, 1981).
27. The Reports of the Secretary General on UNIFIL consistently set forth particulars concerning harassment and incursions including the use of weapons by the *de facto* forces against UNIFIL. In addition, the *de facto* forces have murdered captured UNIFIL soldiers. See, *e.g., Report of the Secretary-General on the United Nations Interim Force in Lebanon* [hereafter cited as *Report*] (for the period 11 Dec. 1979 to 12 June 1980) at 10-15, Doc. S/13994 (12 June 1980); *id.* (for the period 13 June to 11 Dec. 1980) at 13-17, Doc. S/14295 (12 Dec. 1980).
    In *Special Report of the Secretary-General on the United Nations Interim Force in Lebanon* [hereafter cited as *Special Report*], Doc. S/13888 (11 April 1980) a summary appears at p. 5:
    > In the present situation, far too much of UNIFIL's energy is distracted by efforts to resist the harassment and violence to which it is daily exposed, while its capacity to carry out its functions is greatly reduced by the fact that it cannot operate in a vital part of its area of operations which is at present controlled by the *de facto* forces.

civilians wounded.[28] Following the adoption of Security Council resolution 490 on July 21, 1981, which called "for an immediate cessation of all armed attacks," the United States and Saudi Arabian Governments negotiated a cease-fire between the Government of Israel and the PLO which became effective on July 24, 1981.[29] No written text of the agreement has been revealed and it is probable, consequently, that it was oral. At the time the cease-fire was announced, Ambassador Habib and Prime Minister Begin had just met following a meeting of the Israeli Cabinet.[30] According to the New York Times, each then made "a one sentence announcement":

"I have today reported to President Reagan," Mr. Habib said, "that as of 13:30 hours local time July 24, 1981, all hostile military action between Lebanese and Israeli territory in either direction will cease."

Mr. Begin said, "Ladies and gentlemen of the press, the Government of Israel endorsed the statement just made to you by Mr. Philip Habib, the emissary of the President of the United States."[31]

Thereafter, the PLO interpreted the agreement as being applicable only to the area of the Israeli-Lebanese border referred to by Mr. Habib.[32] This is the area in southern Lebanon where the PLO maintained organized military forces under its control. Following Mr. Habib's trip to the Middle East from February 26 to March 9, 1982, Israel claimed that "the cease-fire included attacks against Israeli positions launched from Jordan, Syria, or other areas"[33] and also included any attacks in the occupied territories of the West Bank and Gaza.[34] The subsequent Israeli interpretation, as expressed by its representative in the Security Council on July 6, 1982, was that it was applicable to attacks by the PLO on any Jew which took place anywhere in the world.[35] The Israeli interpretation is based upon the assumed validity of the claim of "the Jewish people" as a transnational nationality entity which is legally linked to the State of Israel.[36] This claim, however, is not accepted in international law which acknowledges the legal relationship between an individual and the state of his normal and regular nationality status.[37] There is no valid doctrine in the present international law which ties

---

28. Cong. Res. Service, *Lebanon: Israeli-Palestinian Confrontation* 32 (Issue Brief IB 81090, Aug. 10, 1982).
29. *Id.*
30. New York Times, July 25, 1981, p. 1, col. 6, cont. p. 4, cols. 3-6 at p. 4, col. 5.
31. *Id.* at p. 4, cols. 5-6.
32. *Supra* note 28 at 34.
33. *Id.*
34. The relevant law applicable to the occupied territories, however, is found in the Geneva P.O.W. and Civilians Conventions, both of 1949, and a bilateral cease-fire could not supercede these treaties even if it had provisions which attempted to do so. These Conventions do not prohibit acts of resistance against the occupant. Geneva P.O.W. Convention, 75 U.N.T.S. 135, 6 U.S.T. & O.I.A. 3316; Geneva Civilians Convention, 75 U.N.T.S. 287, 6 U.S.T. & O.I.A. 3516.
35. *Provisional Verbatim Record of the 2,375th Security Council Meeting,* S/PV 2375, pp. 8-33 at 28-33 (6 June 1982).
36. Mallison, "The Zionist-Israel Juridical Claims to Constitute 'the Jewish People' Nationality Entity and to Confer Membership in It: Appraisal in Public International Law," 32 *Geo. Wash. L. Rev.* 983-1075 (1964).
37. The U.S. Department of State rejected the "Jewish people" claim as a valid concept of international law in the letter from Assistant Secretary of State Talbot of April 20, 1964 to Dr. Elmer Berger, Executive Vice President of the American Council for Judaism. 8 Whiteman, *Digest of Int'l Law* 34-35 (1967).

7

all members of any particular religion to any national state with both rights and responsibilities involved in the claimed allegiance.

The United States interpretation of the cease-fire agreement was expressed by State Department spokesman Dean Fischer during the March 18, 1982 press briefing:

> The cessation of hostilities pertains to all hostile military activity from Lebanon into Israel and vice versa. Therefore, any hostile action originating from Lebanon, but going through Syria and Jordan into Jordan [sic] would be a violation of the ceasefire.
> The same would apply to an Israeli action from Israel into Lebanon transiting international waters or foreign territories.[38]

The U.S. view appears to be inconsistent with the Israeli view that the agreement applied worldwide and within the occupied territories. In an address to the Israeli National Defense College on August 8, 1982 Prime Minister Begin indicated significant differences between the U.S. and Israeli interpretations:

> Even Philip Habib [the U.S. negotiator of the July 24, 1981 cease-fire] interpreted the agreement ending acts of hostility as giving them freedom to attack targets beyond Israel's borders. We have never accepted this interpretation. Shall we permit Jewish blood to be spilled in the Diaspora? Shall we permit bombs to be planted against Jews in Paris, Rome, Athens or London? Shall we permit our ambassadors to be attacked? [39]

A report from Israel appearing in the New York Times of February 10, 1982 stated that Israel had drawn up plans for a large-scale invasion of Lebanon but would not attack except in response to a PLO provocation.[40] The article, cleared by the Israeli military censor, reported that there were differences of opinion within the Government of Israel as to what would constitute adequate provocation. The article stated:

> As described here, Mr. Sharon's plan would be directed against the PLO in an effort to deal a decisive, crippling blow to its military employment in southern Lebanon.[41]

A Reuters' dispatch appearing in the New York Times on February 26, 1982 reported:

> Israel's new Ambassador to the United States warned today that Israel could be forced to take military action in southern Lebanon, declaring "I would almost say it's a matter of time."[42]

A report from Beirut appearing in the Christian Science Monitor on March 18, 1982 described a series of Israeli military operations across the international boundary into southern Lebanon. The article stated:

> Israeli forces appear to have launched a campaign of "brinkmanship shadowboxing" in an attempt to bait the Palestinians into provoking a confrontation in southern Lebanon.
> This is the view held by Western diplomats and neutral UN officials here, who say the latest series of Israeli provocations may be an effort to justify an attack the Israelis cannot otherwise afford to make because of unprecedented international pressure.[43]

---

38. U.S. Dept. State Press Briefing, March 18, 1982 at 13-14.
39. Jerusalem Post, Int'l Ed., Aug. 22-28, 1982, p. 14, cols. 1-5, at col. 5.
40. New York Times, Feb. 10, 1982, p. A1, cols. 2-3.
41. *Id.* at col. 3.
42. *Id.,* Feb. 26, 1982, p. A11, col. 4.
43. Christian Sci. Monitor, Mar. 18, 1982, p. 12, cols. 1-3 at col. 1.

It also reported that:

> UN officials are angered to the point of publicizing recent incidents, hoping it will check the provocation. At the same time, they praise the PLO's "unusual restraint."[44]

On February 16, 1982 the United Nations Secretary-General issued a special report on the UNIFIL which stated, *inter alia:*

> The encroachments established in the UNIFIL area of deployment by the *de facto* forces, which are supported and supplied by Israel, have not been removed, and violations of Lebanon's territorial integrity have also continued.[45]

The report also pointed out that it was a strong recommendation of the force commander, Lieutenant-General Callaghan of Ireland, supported fully by the Lebanese Government, that the size of the UNIFIL should be increased by no less than 1,000 troops in order to enhance its ability to carry out its responsibilities pursuant to Security Council resolution 425.[46] On June 10, 1982 the Secretary-General issued a report on UNIFIL covering the period from December 11, 1981 to June 3, 1982. He provided detailed information on the military operations in southern Lebanon. The main points raised by him were:

> The *de facto* forces continued to maintain encroachments in the UNIFIL area of deployment at Bayt Yahun, Blate, Ett Taibe, Rshaf and on Hill 880 near AtTiri. UNIFIL made intensive efforts, including repeated contacts with the Israeli authorities, to have these provocative positions removed. However, the necessary cooperation was not forthcoming.[47]
>
> * * *
>
> IDF [Israel Defense Forces] activities in the UNIFIL area of operation continued unabated. UNIFIL and UNTSO raised the matter repeatedly with the Israeli authorities.[48]
>
> * * *
>
> There were violations of Lebanese air space by Israeli aircraft and of Lebanese waters by Israeli naval vessels. UNIFIL observed 130 air violations and 62 sea violations in December 1981, 285 air violations and 53 sea violations in January 1982, 121 air violations and 54 sea violations in February, 187 air violations and 97 sea violations in March, 368 air violations and 59 sea violations in April, and 302 air violations and 59 sea violations in May.
>
> During the period under review, various UNIFIL positions and personnel came under close fire by IDF. Seventeen such incidents were reported. Those incidents as well as the repeated violations of Lebanese territory were strongly opposed.[49]

On April 21, 1982 one Israeli soldier was killed by a land mine in the area controlled by the *de facto* forces.[50] Within hours, Israeli aircraft bombed areas along the Lebanese coast for a period of about two hours in supposed retaliation. This was a major breach in the cease-fire of July 24, 1981 and the PLO did not retaliate.[51] The Secretary-General also reported that on May 9, 1982 Israeli aircraft again attacked targets in Lebanon and that later that day UNIFIL observed rockets fired from Palestinian positions into northern Israel.[52] This Palestinian

---

44. *Id.* at col. 2.
45. *Special Report, supra* note 27, at 1, Doc. S/14869 (16 Feb. 1982).
46. *Id.* at 2.
47. *Report, supra* note 27, p. 10, para. 40, Doc. S/15194 (10 June 1982).
48. *Id.*
49. *Id.* at 11, para. 46.
50. *Id.* at para. 45.
51. New York Times, April 22, 1982, p. 14, col. 4.
52. *Supra* note 47, p. 11, para. 50.

response is the only reference to a PLO military response, or indeed to any PLO military action across the Lebanese border against Israel, during the period of the report. The casualties from this particular Israeli bombing were listed as 16 killed and 56 wounded. No Israeli casualties or damage were reported from the PLO response.[53]

Thus the evidentiary record as supplied by the UN forces on the scene shows that during the preceding nine months the PLO did in good faith adhere to the terms of the cease-fire except for the shelling on May 9. There had been no PLO response to the carrying out of Israeli "training maneuvers" with tanks and live ammunition on Lebanese soil near PLO positions, actions called "intensive, excessive and provocative" by UN observers in their official reports.[54]

C. The Attack-Invasion

The incident awaited by Israel occurred on June 3, 1982 when the Israeli Ambassador to Great Britain was critically wounded in an assassination attempt.[55] Israel immediately accused the PLO and the PLO denied responsibility, stating through its London representative that the attack served Israeli interests and not Palestinian ones.[56] The British authorities arrested two Jordanians and an Iraqi and charged them with the crime.[57] An intensive Israeli aerial "reprisal" was already underway by the evening of June 5 when the British representative stated at the United Nations that the attack had in fact been carried out by members of an anti-PLO Arab group, one of whom carried a "hit list" which included the PLO London representative.[58] For two days Israel carried out the heaviest and most sustained air attacks on Lebanon since the July 17, 1981 attack.[59] The PLO responded to this with an artillery and rocket attack on the Galilee area of northern Israel in which, according to Israeli accounts, one person was killed.[60]

---

53. Wash. Post, May 10, 1982, p. A1, cols. 2-3 at col. 2.
54. Quoted by Robin Wright in "Israeli 'provocations' in southern Lebanon fail to goad PLO—so far," Christian Sci. Monitor, March 18, 1982, p. 12, col. 1.
55. Wash. Post, June 5, 1982, p. A1, col. 1. The more basic considerations which led to the attack-invasion are considered in Sheila Ryan, "Israel's Invasion of Lebanon: Background to the Crisis," *Journal of Palestine Studies,* Vol. 11, No. 4 and Vol. 12, No. 1 (combined issue Nos. 44 & 45) p. 23 (Summer and Fall, 1982).

A careful chronology of the attack-invasion, consistent with the facts upon which the present text is based, is Carole Collins, "Chronology of the Israeli Invasion of Lebanon, June-August 1982," *id.* pp. 135-92.
56. Wash. Post, *supra* note 55, p. A22, cols. 1-2 at col. 2.
57. *Id.,* June 6, 1982, p. A30, cols. 5-6.
58. *Provisional Verbatim Record of the 2,374th Security Council Meeting,* S/PV. 2374, p. 11 (5 June 1982). Prime Minister Thatcher affirmed this. Wash. Post, June 8, 1982, p. A1, col. 4, cont. p. A11, cols. 3-6 at p. A11, col. 6.

On June 9, the Associated Press reported that a statement delivered to its Beirut offices signed with a name used by followers of Abu Nidal claimed responsibility for the attack on the Israeli Ambassador in London. Abu Nidal was expelled from the P.L.O. in the early 1970's and was condemned to death by it in 1978. Wash. Post, June 10, 1982, p. A24, col. 3.
59. Wash. Post, June 5, 1982, p. A1, cols. 3-4, cont. p. A24, cols. 1-6, at col. 4.
60. *Id.* at p. A24, col. 3.

Then on June 6 the massive Israeli attack-invasion into Lebanon began and within a week it was estimated that 10,000 people were killed or wounded.[61] The majority of the victims were Palestinian and Lebanese civilians. Some refugee camps, particularly in the south, were completely destroyed. A number of towns and cities were reduced in large measure to rubble. There were PLO offices, ammunition dumps or other facilities in some of the population centers (just as there are Israeli military facilities in Tel Aviv) but there was no attempt to limit the destruction to such facilities.[62] Their superior offensive weapons allowed the Israelis also to knock out the Syrian surface to air missiles in the Bekaa Valley and many Syrian aircraft.[63] By June 9 the attack-invasion had reached the outskirts of Beirut.

Wide World Photos

A bulldozer pushes dirt over a mass grave for Lebanese and Palestinian victims of the combined air and artillery attacks that preceded the Israeli capture of Sidon in June, 1982.

---

61. The textual paragraph is based on numerous, consistent, and cumulative press reports. *E.g.,* "Agony of the Innocents: For Lebanon's civilians, death and suffering are the victors," *Time* magazine, June 28, 1982, pp. 20-21 at p. 20, col. 3; Wash. Post, June 11, 1982, p. A1, col. 5 cont. p. A19, cols. 1-2 at p. A19, col. 2; New York Times, June 13, 1982, p. 12, cols. 5-6 at col. 6.
62. *E.g.,* Wash. Post, June 12, 1982, p. A1, col. 5, cont. p. A20, cols. 1-4, at p. A1, col. 5.
63. "Into the Wild Blue Electronically," *Time* magazine, June 21, 1982, p. 20, col. 2.

A Lebanese family (above) races for shelter as low-flying Israeli jets bomb the seafront residential districts of West Beirut on July, 27, 1982. An Israeli artillery spotter (below) watches smoke from a shell fired by the tank next to his rise from the Palestinian refugee camp of Bourj al-Barajna on the outskirts of West Beirut July 9 as Israelis continue a day-long shelling of Palestinian positions.

II. Aggression and Self-Defense in the World Legal Order

A. The International Law Criteria

Since the responsibility of the world legal order is to exercise effective community control of violence and coercion by national states and other subjects of international law, it protects human and material values by promoting peaceful procedures and deterring aggression.

1. The United Nations Charter Framework

The world legal order is set forth in article 2(3) and (4), and article 51 of the United Nations Charter. These articles provide a codification of the pre-existing customary law concerning aggression and self-defense. Article 2(3) states:

> All members shall settle their international disputes by peaceful means in such a manner that international peace and security are not endangered.

Paragraph 4 of the same article contains the prohibition upon aggression:

> All members shall refrain in their international relations from the threat or use of force against the territorial integrity or political independence of any state, or in any other manner inconsistent with the purposes of the United Nations.

Article 51 of the Charter incorporates the customary law of self-defense in the following words:

> Nothing in the present Charter shall impair the inherent right of individual or collective self-defense if an armed attack occurs. . . .

These articles taken together comprise a minimum order. It is minimum in the sense that it protects only the primary interest in freedom from aggression and the right of self-defense as a sanction.[64] An optimum order, in contrast, includes minimum order and a consensual and nondiscriminatory environment in which individuals may achieve their values or interests.

Article 51 is sometimes interpreted as restricting the "inherent right" of self-defense to situations where an armed attack has in fact taken place. If this interpretation is accepted, anticipatory self-defense is illegal *per se.* The negotiating history at the San Francisco Conference reveals that article 51 was intended to incorporate the entire customary law or "inherent right" of self-defense.[65] This comprehensive incorporation of the customary law includes reasonable and necessary anticipatory self-defense since this is an integral part of the customary law. This negotiating history governs the meaning of the article in each of the five official languages of the Charter. The French text which uses the broad term "aggression armée," encompassing the conception of "armed attack" but not

---

64. McDougal & Feliciano, *Law and Minimum World Public Order* 121-24 and *passim* (1961).
65. 12 *U.N. Conference on Int'l Organization* 680 (1945).

limited to it, is a more accurate reflection of the negotiating history than is the English text if the latter is read out of the context of the negotiations.

2. The United Nations Definition of Aggression

The League of Nations considered the question of defining aggression as early as 1923 in connection with the preparation of a draft Treaty of Mutual Assistance which was abandoned in 1924 for lack of agreement.[66] In 1933 the Soviet Union submitted a detailed proposal listing acts demonstrating aggression at the London Disarmament Conference.[67] This subsequently formed the basis of the Litvinov-Politis definition adopted by the Committee for Security Questions of that Conference and was incorporated in bilateral agreements between the U.S.S.R. and eleven other states.[68]

The framers of the United Nations Charter left the application of "any threat to the peace, breach of the peace, or act of aggression" to the appraisal of the Security Council. Subsequently, when the General Assembly considered the desirability of the formulation of a definition of aggression, various objections were raised.[69] One view was that a definition which would cover all kinds of aggression would be rendered very difficult by the changing techniques of modern warfare and that a definition might, by its omissions, encourage an aggressor or delay action by the Security Council. In addition, those opposed to a definition were concerned about the types of aggression covered including whether or not the definition should concern itself with "indirect aggression." Some concerns were expressed about the doctrine of proportionality, but these were resolved. From an historical perspective, the proportionality doctrine has long been established in customary law and is incorporated in the "inherent right" of self-defense in article 51 of the United Nations Charter.

One of the academic critics of defining aggression, Professor Julius Stone, has conceived the task as "finding a definition of aggression clear and precise enough for certain and automatic applications to all future situations."[70] He has also deplored "the impossibility of containing the unceasing struggle for a minimal justice in international relations within the straitjacket of precise formulae for the definition of aggression."[71] If it is conceived in this manner, he accurately regards the task of definition as impossible.[72] His criticism, however, is based upon a misunderstanding of the function of legal principles, rules and definitions. Their function is not to displace human decision-makers in the Security Council or elsewhere by predetermining particular decisions. It is rather to provide the agreed upon community standards which implement in a more detailed manner the basic criteria of the Charter. It should be obvious that the intelligence and integrity of human decision-makers are required to apply any definition to a particular factual situation. Professor Stone, however, appears to

---

66. C.L. Brown-John, "The 1974 Definition of Aggression: A Query," 15 *Can. Y.B. Int'l L.* 301 (1977).
67. 5 Whiteman, *supra* note 37, at 729-31 (1965).
68. *Id.* at 735-36.
69. The textual paragraph is based in part upon *Definition of Aggression,* U.N. Pub. No. OPI/550 (July, 1975).
70. J. Stone, *Aggression and World Order: A Critique of United Nations Theories of Aggression* 10 (1958).
71. *Id.* at 12.
72. *Id.* and *passim.*

have adhered to the elements of his earlier position even after the General Assembly adopted the Definition of Aggression.[73]

After agreement was reached in the drafting committee, the completed text of the Definition was adopted by the General Assembly on December 14, 1974 by consensus as resolution 3314 (XXIX).[74] There was neither intention nor the authority to modify the wording or meaning of the Charter, and this is enunciated in article 6 of the Definition. The purpose was to provide a more detailed formulation of community criteria than appears in the articles of the Charter.

Article 1 of the Definition states that:

> Aggression is the use of armed force by a State against the sovereignty, territorial integrity or political independence of another State, or in any other manner inconsistent with the Charter of the United Nations....

The last quoted clause concerning inconsistency with the Charter is particularly important. Since the Charter recognizes the rights of peoples[75] as well as states, aggression by a state against a people is also violation of article 1.

Article 2 of the Definition provides:

> The first use of armed force by a State in contravention of the Charter shall constitute *prima facie* evidence of an act of aggression although the Security Council may, in conformity with the Charter, conclude that a determination that an act of aggression has been committed would not be justified in the light of other relevant circumstances, including the fact that the acts concerned or their consequences are not of sufficient gravity.

Article 3 lists certain actions which qualify as acts of aggression. These include, *inter alia,* the invasion by the armed forces of another state; the bombardment by the armed forces of a state against the territory of another state; the blockade of the ports or coasts of a state; and a state allowing a second state to use the first state's territory for an aggression on a third one. Consistent with the customary law, article 3 states that its provisions are applicable "regardless of a declaration of war." Article 4 points out that the prior enumeration of acts is not exhaustive. The Nuremberg Principles[76] concerning the criminal nature of aggression and the illegality of any territorial acquisition resulting from aggression are incorporated in article 5. Article 7 provides that nothing in the Definition prejudices the right to self-determination as enunciated in the Charter and in the Declaration on the Principles of International Law Concerning Friendly Relations and Co-operation among States;[77] and article 8 sets forth the principle that all the provisions of the Definition are interrelated. It is significant that there was no negative vote on this Definition which constitutes the most authoritative formulation of community criteria concerning the prohibition upon aggression.

---

73. Stone, "Hopes and Loopholes in the 1974 Definition of Aggression," 71 *Am. J. Int'l L.* 224 (1977); Stone, *Conflict Through Consensus: United Nations Approaches to Aggression, passim* (1977).

74. *29 U.N. GAOR, Supp. 31* at 142, Doc. A/9631.

75. *U.N. Charter,* Preamble, arts. 1(2), 55, 73, 76, 80(1).

76. U.N. General Assembly resolution 95(I) (1946) recognized by consensus the principles of international law of the Charter and Judgment of the International Military Tribunal at Nuremberg. These principles were codified by the International Law Commission. [1950] *Y.B. Int'l L. Comm.,* Vol. 2, pp. 374-80.

77. G.A. Res. 2625 (XXV), *25 U.N. GAOR, Supp. 28,* at 121-24, Doc. A/8028 (24 Oct. 1970).

3. The Legal Requirements for Self-Defense

The international law which sets forth the criteria for self-defense, and distinguishes it from aggression, has been enunciated and developed by the community of states over a considerable period of time. The objective of these legal doctrines is to ensure freedom from coercion and to protect the inclusive interests or values of all states and peoples in promoting peaceful settlement of international disputes and deterring acts of aggression.

The customary law prescribes the use of peaceful procedures, if they are available, as the first basic requirement of self-defense. The second is an actual necessity as opposed to a sham or pretense, for the use of force in responding coercion, and the third is proportionality in responding coercion.[78] Necessity traditionally has been formulated in narrow and restrictive terms. The policy reason for this apparently has been to avoid an open-ended conception of self-defense which might be employed as a screen for aggression. If the first two requirements for self-defense have been met, and the circumstances require resort to a defensive response involving armed force, the principle of proportionality specifies that the response must be proportional to the character and amount of the initiating coercion.

There are several subsidiary criteria for appraisal of particular aspects of a claimed self-defense situation which give more precise content to the requirements of peaceful procedures, necessity, and proportionality. These include a factual description of the participants, an appraisal of their objectives in terms of their inclusive or exclusive character and whether or not they involve a conservation or extension of values, as well as the relative consequentiality of the values to be protected.[79] These factors must be evaluated favorably before a military action may be appraised as lawful self-defense.

4. Anticipatory Self-Defense

The legal criteria concerning self-defense include reasonable and necessary anticipatory self-defense. Anticipatory self-defense is regarded as a highly unusual and exceptional matter which may only be employed when the evidence shows a threat of imminent armed attack and the necessity to act is overwhelming.[80] The requirements of necessity and proportionality have always been applied with more rigor to a claim of anticipatory self-defense than to a claim of defense against an armed attack.[81]

One of the leading instances in which the legal principle of anticipatory self-defense, which is a part of the "inherent right" referred to in article 51 of the Charter, has been applied is the famous *Caroline* incident[82] which involved a steamer of that name employed in 1837 to transport personnel and equipment from United States territory across the Niagara River to Canadian rebels on Navy Island and then to the mainland of Canada. The British Government (then the

---

78. The textual paragraph is based, in part, on *supra* note 64 at chap. 3. As a practical matter, peaceful procedures are usually more available in the situation of anticipatory self-defense.
79. *Id.* at 167-90.
80. See *e.g.,* 12 Whiteman, *Digest of International Law* 47 (1971). The doctrine of anticipatory self-defense was examined in the *Judgment* in 1 Trial of the Major War Criminals Before the International Military Tribunal at Nuremberg 205-09 (1947). [Hereafter cited as I.M.T.].
81. *Supra* note 64 at 231.
82. 2 Moore, *Digest Int'l Law* 409-14 (1906).

sovereign in Canada) apparently expected that the United States Government would stop the military assistance to the rebels, but the latter did not do so and the *Caroline* remained as a threat to Canada. Thereafter, British troops crossed the Niagara River into the territory of the United States and, after a conflict in which at least two United States nationals were killed, they set the *Caroline* afire and it was wrecked on Niagara Falls. Following the attack on the vessel, the troops immediately returned to Canada without any further military action in the United States. In the ensuing controversy, Great Britian rested its case on the basis of reasonable and necessary anticipatory self-defense. The United States did not deny that circumstances might exist in which Great Britain lawfully could invoke such self-defense, but denied that they existed in this situation. The controversy was terminated, nevertheless, following a British diplomatic apology, but significantly without any British assumption of legal responsibility for the deaths of the two Americans, the wounding of others, and the destruction of the *Caroline*. The absence of further legal claim by the United States should be interpreted as tacit acquiescence in the lawfulness of the British action.

The *Caroline* incident is best known for Secretary of State Webster's formulation of the requirements of self-defense as involving a "necessity of self-defense, [which is] instant, overwhelming, leaving no choice of means, and no moment for deliberation."[83] The quoted wording concerning "no choice of means, and no moment for deliberation" is misleading since, where an actual necessity exists, international law requires a state invoking anticipatory self-defense to go through a process of deliberation resulting in the choice of lawful, that is, proportional, means of responding coercion. In the actual facts of the incident, the British responding coercion was a choice of means which was proportional to the threat posed by the ship.

A more recent incident which is relied upon in customary law arose during the Second World War.[84] Following the Vichy French Government's armistice with Germany in June 1940, many vessels of the French Navy took refuge in Alexandria in Egypt, Oran in French North Africa, or Martinique in the West Indies. In early July, the British presented the French naval commander in each of these locations with proposals setting forth alternatives concerning the disposition of French naval vessels, any one of which was designed to prevent them from coming under German control. The first and preferred proposal was that the French naval vessels join with the Royal Navy in continuing the war against Germany. The second alternative involved the complete demilitarization of the French vessels so that they would be of no use to Germany. The third alternative, which the British emphasized would only be used with great reluctance if the first two were rejected, was that Great Britain would attack and sink the vessels. At Alexandria and Martinique the French naval commanders accepted the second alternative. At Oran the first two alternatives were rejected and after further fruitless negotiations, British naval and air forces attacked and sank or severely damaged the French warships.

If a realistic appraisal is made of the grim realities of the situation confronting Great Britain, the British attack on the warships of its former ally and accompanying incursions into French territorial waters and airspace were justified as anticipatory self-defense. Very little other than British naval and air power stood

---

83. Mr. Webster to Mr. Fox, April 24, 1841, 29 *Brit. & Foreign State Papers* 1129 at 1138 (1840-1841).

84. 1 *Oppenheim's International Law* 303 (8th ed., Lauterpacht, 1955).

between the victorious German armies and successful invasion of the United Kingdom. Acquisition of major elements of the French Navy would probably have made a German invasion possible. The applicable principles of international law did not require the British to defer action until after the French warships were incorporated into the German Navy. Respected international legal authority has appraised the British action as lawful anticipatory self-defense.[85]

The Cuban Missile Crisis of 1962 provides an example of anticipatory self-defense in a nuclear context.[86] As in the two previous instances, the facts were clear, but in this case they were revealed by photographic evidence of intercontinental missile sites being emplaced in Cuba. It will be recalled that when Ambassador Stevenson made them available, these photographs were decisive in changing the climate of opinion, first in the United Nations Security Council and later in the world community. The missiles and the launching sites were being emplaced in secret and in the face of the Soviet diplomatic assurances that no offensive weapons would be placed in Cuba. Because prior diplomatic discussions emphasizing United States opposition to the emplacement of any offensive weapons in Cuba had in fact failed to prevent their positioning, and because of a perceived pressure of time in stopping the emplacement, no further diplomatic efforts were considered feasible. Among the alternative recommendations which were presented to President Kennedy was the proposal to bomb the missile sites. Some international lawyers thought that this would be fully justified in law because of the great danger to the entire Western Hemisphere caused by this Soviet attempt to drastically upset the nuclear balance of power.[87] President Kennedy, however, in invoking national self-defense on October 22, selected a limited naval blockade or quarantine-interdiction as the method to prevent the introduction of further offensive weapons and to bring about the removal of those present. This method permitted the use of diplomatic means at the United Nations and elsewhere and ultimately resulted in the Kennedy-Khrushchev agreement which terminated the missile crisis and led to the withdrawal of the missiles from Cuba.

In appraising whether or not each of the legal requirements had been met in the United States invocation of anticipatory self-defense, it is highly significant that on October 23rd the Organ of Consultation of the Organization of American States invoked collective self-defense on behalf of the Inter-American community. The regional decision-makers dealt with the same fact situation which the United States had dealt with on the previous day and came to the same conclusion that an actual necessity for anticipatory self-defense existed.[88] The Organ of Consultation also approved the specific measures undertaken by the United States, and by the time the limited naval blockade or quarantine-interdiction was ended, there were ships from a number of Latin-American navies participating in the enforcement of the blockade.[89]

The severely limited military measures employed by the United States amounted to the least possible use of the military instrument of national policy. If it had not been successful, somewhat more coercive use of military power could

---

85. *Id.*
86. Mallison, "Limited Naval Blockade or Quarantine-Interdiction: National and Collective Defense Claims Valid Under International Law," 31 *Geo. Wash. L. Rev.* 335-98 (1962).
87. Former Secretary of State Acheson was one such lawyer. R.F. Kennedy, *Thirteen Days: A Memoir of the Cuban Missile Crisis* 37-38 (Signet ed., 1979).
88. *Supra* note 86 at 378-79.
89. *Id.* at 392-94.

be justified under international law. The legal consequence of the restricted use of military force is that the proportionality test in even its most rigorous and extreme form was easily met.[90] In addition to the approval of the United States measures by the Organization of American States, the measures also met with wide approval within the United Nations.

B. Appraisal of Government of Israel Claims Under the Criteria of International Law

1. Claims of the Government of Israel to Lawful Self-Defense

Mr. Blum, the Israeli Permanent Representative at the United Nations, at the meeting of the Security Council on June 6, 1982 specifically claimed that the Government of Israel attack-invasion was justified as lawful self-defense in the following statement:

> It thus becomes imperative for the Government of Israel to exercise its legitimate right of self-defence to protect the lives of its citizens and to ensure their safety.[91]

On the same day, the Government of Israel through Mr. Blum also invoked anticipatory self-defense to "deter" future "terrorism":

> Faced with intolerable provocations, repeated aggression and harassment, Israel has now been forced to exercise its right of self-defence to arrest the never-ending cycle of attacks against Israel's northern border, to deter continued terrorism against Israel's citizens in Israel and abroad, and to instill the basic concept in the minds of the PLO assassins that Jewish life will never again be taken with impunity.[92]

Since the attack-invasion announced as directed against the PLO has violated the territorial integrity of Lebanon, it is appropriate to consider also Mr. Blum's statement claiming Lebanese responsibility for the alleged threat to Israel. He stated concerning Lebanon on June 5:

> If Lebanon is either unwilling or unable to prevent the harbouring, training and financing of PLO terrorists openly operating from Lebanese territory with a view to harassing Israel, Israelis and Jews world-wide, then Lebanon surely must be prepared to face the risk of Israel's taking the necessary countermeasures to stop such terrorist operations.[93]

In connection with this claim against Lebanon, it is important to consider the Government of Israel's prior actions there including, *inter alia,* its support of the *de facto* forces in the south and right-wing militias in the north[94] and its consistent frustration of the United Nations peace-keeping efforts (including those

---

90. *Id.* at 394.
91. *Provisional Verbatim Record of the 2,375th Security Council Meeting,* S/PV. 2375, pp. 8-33, at 17 (6 June 1982). [Provisional Verbatim Records are cited hereafter as S/PV.]
92. *Id.* at 33.
93. S/PV.2374, pp. 27-30 at 30 (5 June 1982).
94. Re the *de facto* forces, see the text accompanying note 26. The New York Times reported on June 17, 1980 that Israel has given more than one billion dollars to the Christian militias in Lebanon. P. 1, cols. 1-2, cont. p. A8, cols. 3-6 at col. 4. Re the connection between Israel and the Phalange, see also Loren Jenkins, "Phalangist Ties to Massacre Detailed," Wash. Post, Sept. 30, 1982, p. A1,cols. 2-4, cont. p. A38, cols. 1-6 at col. 6 where it is stated that during the Lebanese civil war the Gemayal militia (Phalange) was sent to Israel for training under Mossad (Israeli international secret service) and the Israeli Army.

Israeli 320 mm and 175 mm canons (above) fire on beseiged West Beirut after the breakdown of a cease fire on July 7, 1982. Villagers holding a white flag (below) watch an Israeli Centurion tank pass through a village in Southern Lebanon on June 6, the first day of the Israeli invasion.

through UNIFIL).[95] This has resulted in a large measure of Israeli responsibility for the ineffectiveness of the Lebanese Government.

2. The Requirement of Peaceful Procedures

In the event of an actual armed attack of sufficient gravity upon a state, there is no juridical requirement that it resort to peaceful procedures. The lawfulness of its responding coercion need only be appraised under the criteria of necessity and proportionality. If it should be determined that there was no armed attack upon Israel, then it had an obligation to use peaceful procedures in good faith before resorting to coercive measures.

During the winter and spring 1981-82 there were press reports of complaints by Israel to the United States concerning a claimed PLO military build-up in southern Lebanon,[96] and on June 6 in the Security Council meeting Mr. Blum referred to "months of cautioning and warnings."[97] During the same period of time there were concurrent reports of an Israeli build-up near the Lebanese border.[98] In the context of the events which have taken place, it is not possible that the Israeli "cautioning and warnings" can be appraised as meeting the requirement of peaceful procedures. In contrast, Lebanon had used peaceful procedures in February, 1982 in asking the Security Council to obtain Israeli "total and unconditional withdrawal" from Lebanon.[99]

On June 5 and 6 opportunities were provided to the Government of Israel to use peaceful procedures. The Secretary-General of the United Nations reported to the Security Council on June 5 concerning the fact situation. He described eight intensive Israeli air raids on and around Beirut on June 4, and stated that the targets included a Palestinian refugee camp near Beirut on the road to the airport, the Sabra refugee camp, and the area of the Sports Stadium adjacent to it.[100] A large number of refugees from the southern part of Lebanon were camping in the Sports Stadium. He also pointed out that there were heavy exchanges of gunfire in southern Lebanon with the PLO and the Lebanese National Movement on one side and the Israeli armed forces and the *de facto* forces of Major Haddad on the other. He added that he had urged the parties to the conflict "to restore and maintain the cease-fire that had generally held since 24 July 1981."[101]

The Secretary-General reported to the Security Council on the evening of June 6 pursuant to its call in resolution 508 for a cease-fire no later than 0600 hours local time on Sunday, 6 June 1982. He stated that following the adoption of resolution 508 on June 5, the PLO "reaffirmed its commitment to stop all military operations across the Lebanese border."[102] The permanent Representative of Israel, however, informed the Secretary-General on June 5 at 2300 hours New York time (0600 on June 6, Beirut time) that "Israeli reactions were in exercise of its right of self-defense" and that resolution 508, adopted on the previous

---

95. See the text accompanying *supra* note 27.
96. *E.g.,* New York Times, Dec. 5, 1981, p. 26, col. 6.
97. *Supra* note 91 at 33.
98. The U.S. State Dept. had concerns about Israeli military movements near the Lebanese border. See *e.g.,* New York Times April 10, 1982, p. 1, col. 4.
99. S/PV. 2331, pp. 6-10, at 8-10 (23 Feb. 1982).
100. *Supra* note 93, pp. 6-7, at 6.
101. *Id.* at 7.
102. S/PV. 2375, pp. 2-7 at p. 3 (6 June 1982).

day, would be brought to the attention of the Israeli Cabinet.[103] The Secretary-General further reported that subsequent to the scheduled time of the cease-fire Mr. Arafat had informed him that:

> [I]n spite of heavy Israeli air-strikes after the scheduled time of the cease-fire, he had given orders to all PLO units to withhold fire for a further specified period.[104]

These events had taken place prior to the invasion by Israeli ground forces. UNIFIL reported approximately 110 Israeli air strikes which were observed to take place between 0624 and 1435 hours local time on June 6.[105]

Mr. Blum also expressed the attitude of his government toward the Security Council on June 6:

> When is this Council galvanized into action? When Israel, after years of unparalleled restraint finally resorts to the exercise of its right of self-defence, the fundamental and inalienable right of any State, which is also recognized by the United Nations Charter as the inherent right of Members of this Organization. In order to save a terrorist organization from well-deserved and long-overdue retribution, this Council is convened in emergency meetings, urgent meetings and every conceivable form of extraordinary session.[106]
>
> * * *
>
> Given the parliamentary situation in this Organization and the constellation within this Council, Israel cannot expect this body even to deplore PLO barbarism against Israel's civilian population, let alone take any steps with a view to curbing that barbarism.[107]

These views appear to indicate that the Government of Israel would not use peaceful procedures through the United Nations. The Israeli failure to respond affirmatively to the calls for a cease-fire combined with its concurrent continuation of air strikes and the initiating of the attack-invasion amounted to a rejection of the opportunity to use peaceful procedures and thus a failure to comply with this requirement of law.

3. The Requirement of Actual Necessity for Responding Coercion

a. Armed Attack

Even though the PLO is a recognized public body and a national liberation movement representing the people of Palestine[108] and not a state, it is restricted by the customary law of self-defense which is termed "inherent right" in article 51 of the United Nations Charter. Consequently, if there were an armed attack by the PLO against the State of Israel, assuming that the attack was of "sufficient gravity," to use the language of the United Nations Definition of Aggression, it would justify defensive measures by the State of Israel. There is, however, no evidence of an armed attack of any degree of gravity by the PLO. The only PLO use of military force across the Lebanon border against Israel subsequent to the July 24, 1981 cease-fire and prior to the June, 1982 Israeli invasion, according to

---

103. *Id.*
104. *Id.*
105. *Id.* at 4-5.
106. *Id.* at 16.
107. *Id.* at 17.
108. The authoritative analysis of the legal status of the PLO is Kassim, "The Palestine Liberation Organization's Claim to Status: A Juridical Analysis Under International Law," 9 *Denver J. Int'l L. & Policy* 1 (1980).

the UNIFIL report, was PLO responding coercion on May 9 which has been described.[109]

It is also appropriate to enquire as to whether or not the claims made by the Government of Israel through Mr. Blum concerning incidents elsewhere actually constitute an armed attack on Israel by the PLO. Mr. Blum summarized these claims in the Security Council on June 6 as follows:

> [E]ven in the relatively short period of time which has elapsed since the July 1981 agreement on cessation of hostilities, the total of dead and wounded at the hands of the PLO has steadily mounted to a point where it now reaches 17 dead and 241 wounded in a total of 141 terrorist acts all of them originating from terrorist bases inside Lebanon.[110]

Concerning the 17 stated to have been killed, he provided 15 specific examples which included eight Israeli Jews, seven of whom were apparently killed in Israel, and an Israeli diplomat killed in France.[111] He also referred to seven Jews killed in foreign countries including Austria, Belgium, and West Berlin, none of whom were stated to be Israeli citizens.[112] Concerning the seven Israeli Jews stated to be killed in Israel, Mr. Blum said that four were killed on April 22, 1979 and three on April 6, 1980 (both times prior to the cease-fire).[113] The assumption of PLO responsibility in all instances is made without proof being provided. Concerning the Jews outside of Israel, it is also made without the concurrence of the local police authorities in the assumption that the PLO was responsible. The inclusion by Mr. Blum of attacks on non-Israeli Jews outside the State of Israel is consistent with "the Jewish people" nationality claims advanced by the Israeli Government.[114] The Government of Israel has no legal authority to intervene diplomatically on behalf of Jews who are not Israeli nationals. Mr. Maksoud, the permanent observer of the League of Arab States, was the only speaker in the Security Council on June 6 who responded specifically to these claims by Mr. Blum. He stated:

> I am sure that the Jews of the United States, of the United Kingdom, of France, of the Soviet Union, of all the countries in the world reject Israel's claim to be the spokesman for all the Jews in the world and the protector of their rights.[115]

Even if the Jews killed in foreign countries were Israeli nationals, the responsibility for their protection is with the host countries. The Government of Israel would only be entitled to intervene diplomatically if that protection fell below the international law standard.[116] The international law concerning armed attack and aggression relates directly to actions which pose so much danger to the basic interests of a state, including the maintenance of its independence, that the state is justified in using responding military coercion in self-defense. If there were persuasive evidence that the PLO was responsible for all the attacks upon Jews outside Israel, such attacks still could not amount to an armed attack against the State of Israel. To suggest that several isolated attacks on Jews by unidentified

---

109. See the text accompanying *supra* notes 52, 53.
110. *Supra* note 102 at 12-15.
111. *Id.* at 11.
112. *Id.*
113. *Id.* at 9-11.
114. See the text accompanying *supra* notes 35-37.
115. *Supra* note 102, pp. 57-62 at 61.
116. *Supra* note 84 at 686-89.

assailants in Europe present such a danger to the State of Israel is to attempt to trivialize the international law doctrines which deal with actions of great consequentiality endangering the continued existence of a state. Since there was no armed attack against Israel, there cannot be an actual necessity for responding coercion.

After referring to "the cessation of hostilities on the Lebanese border [which] went into effect on 24 July 1981," Mr. Blum continued:

> Violations of the cessation of hostilities began almost immediately and have continued unabated, culminating most recently in the attempted assassination of Ambassador Argov in London.[117]

Mr. Blum specifically accused the PLO of responsibility for the attack on Ambassador Argov in this and other statements. Even if the PLO had been proven, contrary to the facts provided by Scotland Yard,[118] responsible for this shooting, it still would not amount to an armed attack on the State of Israel according to the standards of international law. It is well known that United States ambassadors have been attacked in some countries and, on occasion, killed. On no occasion has the United States Government regarded this as an attack on the United States.

b. Anticipated Armed Attack

Since no actual armed attack or aggression by the PLO upon Israel is involved in the fact situation, it is important to determine whether there existed evidence that any such armed attack was imminent. The striking disparity which the military action showed between the capability of the PLO in southern Lebanon and the Israel armed forces makes improbable the existence of any credible evidence which might reasonably have led Israel to believe that massive responding coercive measures were necessary to prevent an anticipated armed attack.[119] In addition, the consistent refusal of the PLO to respond to Israeli provocations in southern Lebanon (with the one exception) in the several months prior to the Israeli air attacks of June 4, 1982 indicates a PLO effort to avoid a military confrontation with Israel.

Along with including reference to the "Jewish people" nationality claim in his assertion of the Israeli right to lawful self-defense, Mr. Blum also stated the anticipatory self-defense claim as covering "Israel's citizens in Israel and abroad" and "Jewish life" generally.[120] In evaluating any invocation of anticipatory self-defense, the threatened harm must not only be anticipated, but it must be imminent. The *Caroline* and Oran incidents and the Cuban Missile Crisis,[121] already considered as examples of internationally accepted anticipatory

---

117. *Supra* note 35 at 28-30.
118. See the text accompanying *supra* note 58.
119. Analysts at the International Institute for Strategic Studies (London), classify Israel as the fourth strongest military power after the United States, the Soviet Union and China. Jerusalem Post, Int'l Ed., Aug. 8-14, 1982, p. 3, cols. 1-3 at col. 1.

> The war in Lebanon was neither necessary nor inevitable. Even the Likud Government does not pretend that this was a war to defend and preserve Israel's existence. And Ze'ev Schiff, the respected military correspondent of "Ha'aretz" reports that all of the weapons that we captured are barely enough to arm one P.L.O. division.

Shenker, "Why Didn't We Prevent This War?" *New Outlook* (Tel Aviv), Aug.-Sept. 1982, pp. 31-35 at 31, col. 1.
120. *Supra* note 110 at 33. See the text accompanying *supra* notes 36, 37.
121. *Supra* notes 82, 84 and 86.

self-defense, each involved the factually ascertained capability of significant military means being used in the immediate or near future. In the first two incidents the probability of armed attack in the near future necessitated the use of a coercive military response. Because the Cuban Missile Crisis involved a lesser degree of the probability of armed attack in the immediate or near future, even though a nuclear capability was being created, the United States response in anticipatory self-defense did not involve the direct coercive use of armed force but rather a quarantine-interdiction or limited naval blockade.

In striking contrast to the factual clarity and the militarily significant threats posed by these three widely accepted customary law incidents, the alleged PLO threat claimed by Israel was unsupported by convincing evidence and was relatively minor in character. Israeli plans for a large-scale invasion were reported months prior to the actual event and substantiated by Prime Minister Begin's assertion that they awaited only a "clear provocation."[122] Such long term planning for an alleged defensive measure indicates that the claimed threat was not perceived to be imminent. Moreover, after the event, Mr. Begin, in an address on August 8, 1982 to the Israeli National Defense College, said that the Lebanese invasion "does not really belong to the category of wars of no alternative."[123] He stated that it was in response to attacks on civilians and added: "True, such actions were not a threat to the existence of the state."[124] In plain words, he admitted thereby that it was not a war of self-defense. Claims such as those advanced by Israel have not provided sufficient grounds for the legal conclusion of actual necessity in responding to an anticipated armed attack in the past and cannot do so now.

The German attack-invasion of Norway on April 9, 1940 presents an analogy to the Israeli attack-invasion of June 6, 1982. Both involved the attempt to find legal justification in the doctrine of anticipatory self-defense. The detailed German plans, like the Israeli ones, were made over at least a period of several months prior to implementation. The claim made by defendants before the International Military Tribunal (IMT) at Nuremberg was that the German military action was necessary as a defensive measure to forestall a British invasion of Norway. The official diary of the German Naval Operations Staff, however, indicated that this was not the actual perception of German naval officials. An entry of March 23, 1940 records:

A mass encroachment by the English into Norwegian territorial water...is not to be expected at the present time.[125]

---

122. New York Times, Jan. 21, 1982, p. 1, col. 1.
    Further evidence of long term Israeli military preparations for the attack-invasion is the admission by Defense Minister Sharon of a secret visit which he made to Beirut in January, 1982 to reconnoiter the city for a possible Israeli assault. New York Times, August 13, 1982, p. 4, cols. 1-6 at col. 3. Such reconnaissance of the Lebanese capital also raises doubts as to the Israeli claim that their drive into Beirut was not their intention early in the invasion.
123. "The Choice of War: Prime Minister Menachem Begin explains here why Israel decided to launch Operation Peace for Galilee," Jerusalem Post, Int'l Ed., Aug. 22-28, 1982, p. 14, cols. 1-5, at col. 5.
124. Id. See "In the Name of Truth," editorial in New Outlook (Tel Aviv) Aug.-Sept. 1982, at p. 5, col. 1 criticizing false statements by the Government of Israel concerning the attack-invasion of June, 1982.
125. 1 I.M.T. 208.

An Israeli solider (above) guards blindfolded prisoners, with hands and feet bound, arrested June 14, 1982 after Israeli forces occupied Barouk in southeastern Lebanon. In Sidon (below) on July 8 a Palestinian woman asks the whereabouts of her husband of an Israeli soldier outside a detention camp where hundreds of men rounded up during the Israeli advance were held.

26

Other entries indicated a similar perception. The Judgment of the IMT applied the criteria of the *Caroline* incident and stated, *inter alia:*

> It was further argued that Germany alone could decide, in accordance with the reservations made by many of the Signatory Powers at the time of the conclusion of the Kellogg-Briand Pact, whether preventive action was a necessity, and that in making her decision her judgement was conclusive. But whether action taken under the claim of self-defense was in fact aggressive or defensive must ultimately be subject to investigation and adjudication if international law is ever to be enforced.[126]

The International Military Tribunal also considered and rejected the claim that the invasion of Denmark was justified as self-defense and concluded that:

> In the light of all the available evidence it is impossible to accept the contention that the invasions of Denmark and Norway were defensive, and in the opinion of the Tribunal they were acts of aggressive war.[127]

Israel, like Germany, made the claim that it alone could decide whether its military response was necessary. This was not done in words alone, but by the considered action of the Israeli Cabinet on June 6, 1982 in ordering the implementation of the plan for the attack-invasion in the face of unanimous disapproval by the Security Council.[128]

4. The Requirement of Proportionality in Responding Defensive Measures

Since Israel has not met the requirements of either good faith use of peaceful procedures or of actual necessity for responding coercion, it is not necessary to inquire as to the proportionality of the attack-invasion. It may, nevertheless, be useful to consider whether this requirement has been met. The proportionality doctrine appraises the character of responding coercion. The responding measures must be proportional, both in kind and amount, to the character of the threat which is claimed to justify anticipatory self-defense. In what are probably the most important words of Secretary of State Webster in the *Caroline* incident, he stated the requirement of proportionality in these terms: "Nothing unreasonable or excessive [is permitted], since the act, justified by the necessity of self-defense, must be limited by that necessity and kept clearly within it."[129]

Professors McDougal and Feliciano have enunciated the fundamental character of the principle:

> [T]he principle of proportionality is seen as but one specific form of the more general principle of economy in coercion and as a logical corollary of the fundamental community policy against change by destructive modes. Coercion that is grossly in excess of what, in a particular context, may be reasonably required for conservation of values against a particular attack, or that is obviously irrelevant or unrelated to this purpose, itself constitutes an unlawful initiation of coercive or violent change.[130]

It is unfortunate to have to deal with human casualties as a statistical matter. Nevertheless, it is necessary to respond to Mr. Blum's undocumented statistical

---

126. *Id.*
127. *Id.* at 209.
128. *Supra* note 102, pp. 8-33 at 33.
129. *Supra* note 83.
130. *Supra* note 64 at 241-44.

claims before the Security Council citing the 17 alleged victims of the PLO.[131] If Israel's extended interpretation of the cease-fire were accepted for purposes of analysis, the statistics on Palestinian and Lebanese victims of Israeli attacks, wherever they occurred, must also be considered on the same basis. During the time span from the cease-fire through June 3, 1982 one PLO diplomat was killed in Rome by unknown assailants,[132] 16 Palestinian civilians (including at least 11 teenagers and one eight-year-old) were killed by Israeli soldiers or settlers in the West Bank or Gazza,[133] and at least 39 Palestinians and Lebanese were killed in Israeli air attacks on Lebanon.[134] In contrast to the Jewish casualties claimed by Mr. Blum where no evidence of PLO responsibility was produced, all of the Palestinian (with the exception of the diplomat in Rome) and Lebanese casualties were clearly caused by Israeli armed forces or by settlers armed by the Government of Israel. In addition to these earlier reported victims, there were thousands of civilian casualties, both Lebanese and Palestinian, reported since the Israeli attack began on June 4, 1982.[135]

During the Security Council consideration of the events beginning June 5, 1982, no member of the Council and no speaker who was invited to make a statement to the Council supported the view that the Israeli actions met the criteria of proportionality. Ireland (one of the non-permanent members of the Council) spoke to the issue through its permanent representative, Mr. Dorr. On June 5, in the context of the Israeli air attacks but before the beginning of the ground invasion, Mr. Dorr expressed his and his government's deep sympathy over the attack on Ambassador Argov who was accredited concurrently as Ambassador to Ireland. He then continued:

> But we see no justification for, and no correspondence, no relation, between that outrage and the large-scale Israeli raids on the Lebanese capital.
> According to reports, scores of people have been killed in those raids. This was an indiscriminate attempt at retribution. It was on a massive scale and it has killed many who can have had no knowledge of, and no connexion, and indeed no sympathy, with whatever group or individuals planned the attack on the Ambassador.[136]

On June 8, after the massive character of the attack-invasion had become clear, Mr. Dorr returned to the subject of proportionality:

> Where is the correspondence, where is the sense of proportion?
> I do not know exactly the total number of lives lost in attacks on Israel across its borders, or in attacks on Israeli citizens elsewhere over recent years. But I am very sure that the total of lives lost and casualties suffered in all such attacks over recent years is

---

131. Notwithstanding Mr. Blum's claims, the New York Times reported the killing of only three Israelis during the period from the July 24, 1981 ceasefire through June 3, 1982 when Ambassador Argov was attacked: 2 soldiers—one in Gaza (New York Times, March 26, 1982, p. 4, col. 1) and one in south Lebanon (*Id.*, April 22, 1982, p. 1, col. 6)—and one Israeli diplomat in Paris (*Id.*, April 4, 1982, p. 3, col. 1).
132. Wash. Post, Oct. 10, 1981, p. A20, col. 1.
133. New York Times, Dec. 8, 1981, p. 6, col. 3; *id.,* March 21, 1982, p. 1, col. 6; *id.,* March 23, 1982, p. 1, col. 3; *id.,* March 25, 1982, p. 1, col. 2; *id.,* April 9, 1982, p. 10, col. 4; *id.,* April 12, 1982, p. 1, col. 3; *id.,* April 14, 1982, p. 9, col. 1; *id.,* April 17, 1982, p. 3, col. 1; *id.,* April 30, 1982, p. 3, col. 1; *id.,* May 5, 1982, p. A3, col. 4.
134. At least 23 on April 21 (Wash. Post, April 22, 1982, p. 1, col. 6), and 16 on May 9 (*Id.,* May 10, 1982, p. A1, col. 2).
135. *Supra* note 61 and accompanying text.
136. *Supra* note 93, pp. 11-12 at 12.

less than the deaths and injuries caused by the recent major Israeli air attacks on Beirut. Yet we are talking now about a war in which these air raids in turn are merely one aspect of a larger attack on Lebanon.[137]

On June 18 Mr. Dorr reemphasized the importance of the proportionality issue.[138] Mr. Blum was the only person present who expressed a view inconsistent with that of the Irish representative. He characterized Mr. Dorr's statement as "Yet another expression of his well-known tendency to adopt a blinkered, selective, one-sided and lopsided position on the matter before us, as well as on other issues affecting my country."[139]

In summary, this Israeli military action, which according to the Secretary-General initially consisted of "more than two mechanized divisions with full air and naval support,"[140] cannot possibly be appraised as a proportional response to the incidents claimed by Mr. Blum as the justification for the attack-invasion. Neither the customary law nor the provisions of the United Nations Charter nor any other juridical source could provide legal authority for the Israeli military actions. Even the application of the most liberal formulation of the requirement of proportionality would fail to find that it has been satisfied.

C. The Character of the Attack-Invasion Under the Juridical Criteria

The Government of Israel may not successfully invoke the claim of lawful self-defense unless it meets each of the three established criteria which have been considered. Since it has not met any one of the three, it follows, *a fortiori,* that the attack-invasion must be an act of aggression. There are further reasons which also compel this conclusion.

The relevant claims and counter-claims which have been considered took place in the context of the adoption of Security Council resolution 508 on June 5 and of Security Council resolution 509 on June 6. The final preambular paragraph in resolution 508 reaffirmed and supported the statement made by the President and members of the Security Council on June 4, 1982 and the "urgent appeal" issued by the Secretary-General on June 4, 1982. Both of these statements were intended to prevent the Israeli attack-invasion which began on June 6. In the first operative paragraph of resolution 508 the Council:

> *Calls upon* all the parties to the conflict to cease immediately and simultaneously all military activities within Lebanon and across the Lebanese-Israeli border and no later than 0600 hours local time on Sunday, 6 June 1982.

The second operative paragraph asks member states to use their influence to achieve a cessation of hostilities, and the third and final operative paragraph asks the Secretary-General to "undertake all possible efforts" to ensure implementation and compliance with the resolution.

---

137. S/PV. 2377, pp. 11-13 at 12.
138. S/PV. 2379, pp. 6-13 at 7 (18 June 1982).
139. *Id.,* pp. 46-61 at 58-60.
140. *Supra* note 102, pp. 2-7 at 6.

Security Council resolution 509 was adopted on June 6 after it had become clear beyond any possible doubt that Israel had commenced its attack-invasion. In the first operative paragraph the Security Council stated that it:

> *Demands* that Israel withdraw all its military forces forthwith and unconditionally to the internationally recognized boundaries of Lebanon.

The second operative paragraph demanded that the terms of operative paragraph 1 of resolution 508 be strictly observed by all parties. The third operative paragraph called upon the parties to communicate their acceptance of the present resolution to the Secretary-General within twenty-four hours.

It will be recalled that the PLO responded affirmatively to the Security Council's call for the cease-fire enunciated in resolution 508, but that the Government of Israel did not.[141] This provides further evidence, if any should be required, of the aggressive character of the attack-invasion. Since it also was "the first use of armed force by a State in contravention of the Charter" it is a *prima facie* act of aggression as enunciated in article 2 of the United Nations Definition of Aggression.[142]

Resolution 509 was drawn in careful and understated terms so as not to bring about a negative vote by the United States and thus block Security Council action. While the United States Government had demonstrated willingness to vote for the basic principles enunciated in resolutions 508 and 509, it was not willing to even consider, much less to adopt, enforcement measures which were indispensable to stop the attack-invasion. The Spanish draft resolution of June 8, 1982 in a preambular paragraph took note of "The two positive replies to the Secretary-General of the Government of Lebanon and the Palestine Liberation Organization...." The first and fifth draft operative paragraphs provided that the Security Council:

> 1. *Condemns* the non-compliance with resolutions 508 (1982) and 509 (1982) by Israel....
>
> 5. *Demands* that within six hours all hostilities must be stopped in compliance with Security Council resolutions 508 (1982) and 509 (1982) and decides, in the event of non-compliance, to meet again to consider practical ways and means in accordance with the Charter of the United Nations.[143]

The intervening operative paragraphs urged compliance with the Hague Regulations of 1907 and repeated the demand concerning Israeli military withdrawal as well as reiterating adherence to the cease-fire enunciated in paragraph 1 of resolution 508. When the vote was taken, all of the members of the Council voted in favor except for the United States which voted against.[144] The massive character of the military action was evident for all to see on June 8, and following the United States negative vote the Government of Israel continued its military operations.

One of the criteria of the customary law which is used to appraise military action as either defensive or aggressive is whether it reflects the inclusive values of the world community or only the exclusive values of a particular state or public

---

141. *Supra* notes 102-104 and accompanying text.
142. The text accompanying *supra* note 75.
143. U.N. Doc. S/15185 in Appendix C.
144. *Supra* note 137, at pp. 8-10 Ze'ev Schiff [military editor of Ha'aretz], "The Green Light," *Foreign Policy,* no. 50, p. 73 (1983) sets forth the evidence leading to his conclusion of United States acquiescence in the attack-invasion.

body.[145] The inclusive values of the world community in stopping the attack-invasion and returning to peaceful procedures have been set forth authoritatively in Security Council resolutions 508 and 509. The attack-invasion was in no way consistent with those common interests or values and it, at most, reflected the exclusive perceived interests of the Government of Israel. However, it is appropriate to question whether this promotes *bona fide* Israeli interests as opposed to the implementation of the Zionist militarism and expansionism manifested by the Israeli political elite.[146] That which is most urgently needed by the State of Israel and Israelis is the same thing which is most urgently needed by other states and peoples in the Middle East. It is the achievement of a genuine peace based upon justice for all of the peoples of the area and a termination of the continuing conflict situation perpetuated by the policies of the Government of Israel.

It is also necessary, using the same customary law criteria, to inquire as to whether the claimant to self-defense is conserving its existing values or seeking to extend its values at the expense of others.[147] One of the most basic elements in the law of self-defense is that it only authorizes a defender to preserve its existing values and not to acquire those of any enemy even if the enemy is characterized as the attacker in the particular military context.[148] This principle is reflected in Security Council resolution 242 in which "the inadmissibility of the acquisition of territory by war" is emphasized.[149] Because of the absence of either an armed attack or the threat of one against Israel, the extension of its military power and political control throughout southern Lebanon demonstrates aggressive rather than defensive action. Some thoughtful critics have pointed out that the attack-invasion is not a meaningful method to conserve the legitimate Israeli interest in protecting the inhabitants of the Galilee from attack across the Lebanese border. Mr. Anthony Lewis, writing on June 7, 1982 stated:

> To protect Israelis in the Galilee from rockets and shells is essential. But the best method of doing so is the one that U.S. envoy Philip Habib negotiated last July: a cease-fire between Israel and the P.L.O. In terms of keeping northern Israel free of artillery attacks, that arrangement has been astonishingly successful.
>
> * * *
>
> In short, the cease-fire kept the Galilee safe until Israel bombed Lebanon. The argument that aggressive new military action was needed to keep the rockets out turns reality upside-down.[150]

Repeated Government of Israel official statements have declared that Israel does "not covet a square inch of Lebanese soil."[151] It should also be pointed out that the original Israeli justification only claimed the freedom to establish a 25 mile zone in southern Lebanon so that the Galilee would be free from artillery

145. McDougal & Feliciano, *supra* note 64 at 182-83.
146. See S. Tillman, *American Interests in the Middle East,* Chap. 3, "Israel: The Politics of Fear" (1980).
147. *Supra* note 145 at 181-82.
148. R. Y. Jennings, *The Acquisition of Territory in International Law* (1963), Chap. 4, "Title and Unlawful Force."
149. *22 U.N. SCOR,* pp. 8-9 (22 Nov. 1967).
150. New York Times, June 7, 1982; p. A-19, cols. 5-6 at col. 5.
151. Moshe Arens (Israeli Ambassador to the U.S.), "What We Want in Lebanon," Wash. Post, June 11, 1982, p. A15, cols. 1-3, at col. 2.

and rocket attacks.[152] Promptly thereafter, the Israeli military forces went far beyond that limit and soon were at the outskirts of Beirut and then in the city.

In addition, the fact that the Government of Israel has been in southern Lebanon either directly or indirectly through the *de facto* forces since 1978[153] tends to diminish the credibility of the official statements concerning the limited character of the operation and the further assurances concerning early withdrawal. It is also relevant to recognize that the earlier Zionist and Israeli statements concerning the lack of territorial ambitions have proven to be false. The first was the Zionist Organization/Jewish Agency acceptance of the boundaries provided for the State of Israel under the Palestine Partition Resolution followed by attacks upon Palestinians outside of those boundaries as well as within[154] for a period of time before the claimed "invasion" by the Arab armies. Israeli participation in the tripartite invasion of Egypt of 1956 was originally stated to be only for the purpose of defending against fedayeen attacks.[155] It is well known that only President Eisenhower's stated intention to invoke sanctions compelled Israeli withdrawal in early 1957.[156] The same familiar pattern of initial claims of self-defense followed by territorial agrandizement was followed in the intense hostilities of June 1967.[157] More recently, the Government of Israel has claimed to annex the Golan Heights and East Jerusalem through municipal law[158] in violation of the fundamental rule of international law prohibiting the acquisition of territory by conquest reflected in Security Council resolution 242.[159] The consistent history just summarized provides convincing evidence of the expansion of Israeli perceived interests or values as opposed to their conservation.

Following the Second World War, the United Kingdom, the United States, the Soviet Union, and the French Republic wrote the Charter of the International Military Tribunal[160] which was subsequently applied in the trial of the major German defendants at Nuremberg. The Charter provided for individual criminal responsibility where evidence indicated the commission of crimes against peace, war crimes, or crimes against humanity. Article 6(A) provided:

---

152. *Supra* note 102, pp. 8-33 at 33.

   Christopher Walker, "How Peace in Galilee Became the War in Beirut," The Times (London), Aug. 14, 1982, p. 8, cols. 2-5 sets forth the inconsistent official explanations and the consistent evidence of long-range planning.

   Reserve General Aharon Yariv, former Israeli head of military intelligence and currently Director of the Center for Strategic Studies, Tel Aviv University, said: "I know in fact that going to Beirut was included in the original military plan." Jerusalem Post, Int'l Ed., Oct. 3-9, 1982, p. 15, cols. 1-5 at col. 2.

153. The text accompanying *supra* notes 25-27.

154. *E.g.,* the implementation of "Plan D" involving attacks upon Palestinians throughout the Palestine Mandate prior to the "invasion" by the Arab armies is described in Netanel Lorch, *One Long War: Arab Versus Jew Since 1920,* pp. 40-48 under heading "Jewish Forces Take the Initiative" (1976).

155. *E.g.,* Kennett Love, *Suez: The Twice-Fought War* 481 and *passim* (1969).

156. 36 *U.S. Dept. State Bull.* 387 at 389 (Mar. 11, 1957).

157. *Supra* note 155 at 690 and *passim*.

158. Golan Heights Law (Dec. 14, 1981), 21 *Int'l Legal Materials* 214 (1982) [Text provided by Israel Embassy, Wash. D.C.].

159. The text accompanying *supra* note 149.

160. 1 I.M.T. 10-16.

CRIMES AGAINST PEACE: namely, planning, preparation, initiation or waging of a war of aggression, or a war in violation of international treaties, agreements or assurances, or participation in a Common Plan or Conspiracy for the accomplishment of any of the foregoing.

The International Military Tribunal (IMT) considered the basic ideological premises of the Nazi movement including its emphasis on the acquisition of territory by force, its assumption of German racial identification and its claimed superiority to other races.[161] It then recounted the careful planning and carrying out of aggression in the numerous specific instances in which it occurred. It characterized the seizures of both Czechoslovakia and Austria as acts of aggression.[162] The attacks-invasions against Poland, Denmark, Norway, Belgium, the Netherlands, Luxembourg, Yugoslavia, and Greece, *inter alia,* were adjudged also to be acts of aggression.[163] The IMT ultimately held that eight members of the German political and military elite were guilty of crimes against the peace.[164]

Justice Robert Jackson, the United States prosecutor at the IMT, pointed out in the opening statement for the prosecution that the standards to which German defendants would be held would also be the standards later applied to others.[165] It is therefore appropriate to apply the criteria of the IMT to the actions of the Government of Israel in Lebanon.

As in the situation of the Nazi-German elite, that which is done by the Zionist-Israel elite is more important than what is said or planned. A plan of aggression, unless it is acted upon, is not an act of aggression. The long prepared Zionist-Israel plans for aggression against Lebanon were only partially implemented between 1978 and June, 1982. The attack-invasion which began on June 6, 1982 was an act of aggression against both the PLO and the Republic of Lebanon under the existing criteria of international law including the Judgment of the IMT.

Wide World Photos

An Israeli tank (right) in the port district of East Beirut lowers its cannon to turn back an international Red Cross convoy seeking to bring flour and other foodstuffs into besieged West Beirut on July 16, 1982.

---

161. *Id.* at 174-76 and *passim.*
162. *Id.* at 192-98.
163. *Id.* at 198-213.
164. Goring, Hess, Ribbentrop, Keitel, Rosenberg, Raeder, Jodl, and Von Neurath. *Id.* at 366-67.
165. 2 I.M.T. 98-155 at 101.

Israeli soldiers (above) tie the hands of Palestinians behind their backs and make them lie face to the ground in a field on the outskirts of Tyre, southern Lebanon on June 9, 1982, the fourth day of the Israeli invasion of Lebanon. In Sofar, on the Beirut-Damascus highway (below), a blindfolded, wounded Syrian prisoner receives water from an Israeli soldier after a three-day battle for control of the highway in late June.

34

III. The Humanitarian Law for the Protection of Prisoners of War, Wounded and Sick Combatants, and of Civilian Persons and Objects

A. The Historical Development of the Law

International armed conflict has been characterized historically by the extensive destruction of both human and material values. It is a factual situation of varying degrees of violence conducted by states and other participants including organized resistance movements. The international humanitarian law of armed conflict, traditionally known as the law of war, has been developed by the community of states in order to eliminate, or at least minimize, unnecessary destruction. It is designed to impose limitations upon the kinds and degrees of violence and to the extent that the law is effective, a situation of international armed conflict becomes a system of controlled coercion.

The effective sanctioning and enforcement of the law of armed conflict, like that of other branches of international law and of municipal law, is dependent in large measure for its observance upon the common interests of the participants.[166] The group participants include states and their typically regular armed forces, and organized resistance movements and their typically irregular armed forces. If the law is to be effective in imposing restraints upon these groups, it must provide inducements to bring their individual combatants within the juridical system of rights and duties. The futility of attempting to put irregular combatants outside the law is illustrated by the barbaric methods employed against them during the Second World War by the Nazis and the Japanese militarists. Torture and the death penalty were demonstrated to be failures as deterrent sanctions to prevent resistance by irregular forces.[167]

During the Crusades, Western rulers and armies had contact with the Eastern humanitarianism exemplified by Saladin.[168] They were so unfamiliar with humanitarianism in the context of armed conflict that they initially mistook Saladin's compassion for war victims as an indication of military weakness. In contrast, there was little or no influence of humanitarianism in the European wars during the Middle Ages. The Code of Chivalry provided some protection for warriors of high social position, but the code was inapplicable to peasant foot soldiers, civilians, and to enemy personnel of different religious identification.[169]

---

166. W.T. Mallison, *Studies in the Law of Naval Warfare* 19-22 (U.S. Naval War College, 1966).

167. Mallison & Mallison, "The Juridical Status of Irregular Combatants Under the International Humanitarian Law of Armed Conflict," 9 *Case Western Reserve J. Int'l L.* 39-78, at 41 (1977).

168.   If the taking of Jerusalem were the only fact known about Saladin, it were enough to prove him the most chivalrous and great-hearted conqueror of his own, and perhaps of any age.

   S. Lane-Poole, *Saladin and the Fall of the Kingdom of Jerusalem* 234 (1964).

169. M. Keen, *The Laws of War in the Late Middle Ages* 82-100 (1965).

The origin of the customary law prohibition of direct attack upon the civilian population in the Western world should be credited to Hugo Grotius who, in his famous book, *De Jure Bellis ac Pacis,*[170] published in 1625, made the basic distinction between civilians and combatants and recommended humane treatment for prisoners of war.

A more recent historical basis for the contemporary humanitarian law of armed conflict may be found in Lieber's Code (named for its principal author, Professor Francis Lieber of Columbia College, New York) which President Lincoln promulgated to the United States Army as General Order No. 100 in 1863.[171] The Civil War in the United States involved widespread hostilities over a period of four years, and there would have been a much greater destruction of both human and material values if the United States Government had treated every soldier of the armies in rebellion as a traitor under domestic law. In addition, the existence of Lieber's Code encouraged the Confederate forces to adhere to at least the minimal standards of the law of war on the basis of reciprocity and mutuality in observance. The most enduring feature of this Code is that, although it was designed for use in a civil war, it has provided the significant background for the entire modern law of land warfare. Since its provisions included the most enlightened features of the then existing international law of war, it greatly influenced the Brussels Declaration of 1874.

The Brussels Conference of 1874, the first multilateral conference to consider the law of land warfare, met at the invitation of the Russian Czar. The Declaration[172] produced at this Conference has been accorded insufficient attention by most legal scholars because it remained unratified. It comprises, nevertheless, the foundation upon which the modern law of land warfare has been built. Prior to the meeting of the First Hague Conference in 1899, the consensus of the Brussels Conference was widely accepted as the authoritative statement of the customary law on the subject.[173]

Article 9 of the Declaration provided that irregular combatants who meet four conditions are lawful combatants and also provided that they are entitled to prisoner of war status upon capture. Articles 12 and 13 dealt with the legal limitations upon the method of injuring the enemy. Article 13(e) forbade "the employment of arms, projectiles, or material calculated to cause unnecessary suffering." Other articles imposed limitations upon seiges and bombardments and provided protections for prisoners as well as for sick and wounded combatants.

The Brussels Declaration was signed by the representatives of all of the states participating in the Conference, but since it was not ratified by their respective governments, it did not become binding as a multilateral treaty. However, it was the basis for Hague Conventions No. II of 1899[174] and No. IV of 1907.[175] Both the

---

170. An English translation is in 2 *Classics of International Law* (Carnegie Endowment for Int'l Peace, Kelsey transl., 1925).
171. Schindler & Toman (eds.), *The Laws of Armed Conflicts: A Collection of Conventions, Resolutions and Other Documents* 3 (1981).
172. *Id.* at 25.
173. The Russian circular diplomatic note of Dec. 30, 1898 stated that one of the purposes of the Hague Conference of 1899 was to be "the revision of the declaration concerning the laws and customs of war elaborated in 1874 by the Conference of Brussels, and not yet ratified." *Id.* at 57.
174. 32 U.S. Stat. 1803, *supra* note 171 at 57-92.
175. 36 U.S. Stat. 2277, *supra* note 171 at 57-92.

1899 Convention II and the 1907 Convention IV employed a form which included a preamble, a body of the Convention containing important administrative matters, and regulations annexed to the Convention containing the substantive rules of land warfare. These Conventions are considered as embodying the customary international law binding on all states, whether or not they are parties to the Conventions.[176] Their articles 42 through 56 concern military authority over hostile territory and specifically define occupation. They repeat many of the Brussels provisions concerning protections for the human rights of noncombatants as well as basic protections for prisoners of war, and they also repeat the Brussels criteria for irregular combatants.

During the Second World War, even the limited provisions of Hague Convention No. IV and its Annexed Regulations, along with the customary law, were violated by the practices of both the Nazis and the Japanese militarists. Following the conclusion of that war the International Military Tribunal at Nuremberg[177] and the International Military Tribunal for the Far East at Tokyo[178] were established under charters which provided for individual criminal responsibility for violations of the conventional and customary law. The major German and Japanese defendants whose guilt was established clearly were subjected to criminal penalties. Other trials involving individual criminal responsibility took place in national courts where the same criteria of international law were applied.[179]

The Geneva Diplomatic Conference of 1949 met in the shadow of those grim events and aimed at preventing the repetition of the horrors which characterized the recent war. The four Geneva Conventions for the Protection of War Victims which were produced are currently effective multilateral agreements with almost as many state-parties as the United Nations. The first two Conventions[180] provide for the protection of sick, wounded, and shipwrecked military personnel, and the third concerns protections for prisoners of war.[181] The fourth, the Geneva Convention for the Protection of Civilian Persons,[182] was an entirely new convention, expanding in great detail the customary law and Hague protections for civilians and specifying a more comprehensive concept of belligerent occupation. The State

---

176. The International Military Tribunal at Nuremberg held that the Hague Regulations were declaratory of the customary law. *Judgment,* 1 I.M.T. 171 at 254 (1947).
177. Trial of the Major War Criminals Before the International Military Tribunal at Nuremberg (42 vols. 1947-1949).
178. Proceedings of the International Military Tribunal for the Far East (Apr. 29, 1946-Apr. 16, 1948) (approx. 50,000 typewritten pages with separate volume for each day of the trial).
179. See, *e.g.,* U.N. War Crimes Comm., Law Reports of Trials of War Criminals (15 vols., 1947-1949).
180. Convention (I) for the Amelioration of the Condition of the Wounded and Sick in Armed Forces in the Field, 75 U.N.T.S. 31, *supra* note 171 at 305; Convention (II) for the Amelioration of the Condition of Wounded, Sick, and Shipwrecked Members of Armed Forces at Sea, 75 U.N.T.S. 85, *supra* note 171 at 333.
181. Convention (III) Relative to the Treatment of Prisoners of War, 75 U.N.T.S. 135, *supra* note 171 at 355.
182. Convention (IV) Relative to the Protection of Civilian Persons in Time of War, 75 U.N.T.S. 287, *supra* note 171 at 427. (Each of these four Geneva Conventions is dated 12 August 1949.)

of Israel and each of the other states which have been parties to the recurring conflicts with it are parties to the four Geneva Conventions of 1949.[183] On three occasions, beginning in 1969, the PLO has officially stated its adherence to the four Geneva Conventions.[184]

B. The Geneva Prisoners of War Convention (1949)

1. The Legal Criteria for Combatants

The criteria for the juridical status of privileged combatants which entitles the individual to exercise violence lawfully and to have the privileged status of prisoner of war (P.O.W.) if captured, were first set forth in the Brussels Declaration.[185] These criteria are operating under military command, wearing a distinctive sign, carrying arms openly, and complying with the laws and customs of war. The same criteria were repeated in Hague Conventions II and IV concerning land warfare. They were incorporated by reference without amplification into the Geneva Prisoners of War Convention of 1929[186] which provided a more detailed body of rules concerning the treatment of P.O.W.s after capture than did the brief articles of the Hague Regulations on the same subject. The P.O.W. Convention written at Geneva in 1949 went far beyond this in specifying a comprehensive body of rules governing the treatment of P.O.W.s and also developed the law concerning the juridical status of privileged irregular combatants by, *inter alia,* including organized resistance movements.

The inhabitants of many of the states overrun by the German and Japanese armies during World War II continued military resistance through irregular or partisan forces which employed guerrilla methods of warfare. Such irregulars were typically executed upon capture without regard to whether or not they complied with article 1 of the Hague Regulations.[187] The International Committee of the Red Cross (I.C.R.C.) attempted with great persistence, but with little success, to obtain the privileged status of P.O.W.s for those irregulars who met the Hague

---

183. The Government of Israel ratified the four Geneva Conventions of 12 August 1949 on July 6, 1951. *Supra* note 171 at 491. The only reservation made by Israel was concerning its intention to use as its distinctive sign the Red Shield of David rather than one of the signs authorized by article 38 of Geneva Convention I. *Id.* at 506. Lebanon ratified the four Conventions without reservation on April 10, 1951.

184. The first was in a letter of May 6, 1969 from the President of the Palestine Red Crescent Society to the Swiss Federal Political Department (the depositary) in which the adherence was stated to be "on condition of reciprocity." T. Meron [former Legal Adviser of the Israeli Foreign Ministry], *Some Legal Aspects of Arab Terrorists' Claims to Privileged Combatancy* 19 (Sabra Books, Tel Aviv, 1970). This instance and a renewed declaration of December, 1974 are referred to in A. Rosas, *The Legal Status of Prisoners of War* 208 (Helsinki, 1976). On June 7, 1982 the Permanent Observer of the P.L.O. at the United Nations in Geneva sent letters of adherence to the four Geneva Conventions and to Geneva Protocol I Concerning International Armed Conflicts (1977) and to Geneva Protocol II Concerning Non-International Armed Conflicts (1977) to the Swiss Federal Political Department and to the President of the I.C.R.C. Protocols I and II, which are supplementary to the Geneva Conventions of 1949, are in Schindler & Toman, *supra* note 171, at 551 and 619 respectively.

185. *Supra* note 172.

186. 118 U.N.T.S. 343, 47 U.S. Stat. 2021, *supra* note 171 at 271.

187. *U.S. v. Ohlendorf* ("The Einsatzgruppen Case"), 4 U.S. Trials of War Criminals, 1 (1949).

criteria.[188] The Geneva Diplomatic Conference of 1949 met with a full awareness that the organized resistance movements had fought on the side of the Allied Powers. In both the Conference and in the preparatory work leading to it there was a strong disposition to expand the privileged status of irregulars beyond that enunciated in the Hague Regulations.

At the Diplomatic Conference of 1949 a British delegate proposed that the criteria which the Hague Regulations laid down for irregulars be made specifically applicable to regulars of an unrecognized government or authority covered by article 4A (3).[189] However, Committee II of the Diplomatic Conference did not deem it necessary to state expressly that these criteria were applicable to such regular armed forces because the matter of applicability to all regulars was so well established in customary law that a treaty provision would have been superfluous.[190] There was no suggestion that it was necessary to provide specifically that the four criteria apply to regulars of recognized governments covered by article 4A(1). The result was to retain, and to rely upon, the customary law application to regulars of recognized and unrecognized governments and authorities of the same criteria which applies to irregulars. Article 4 also provides that P.O.W. status is extended to those specified persons "who have fallen into the power of the enemy," thereby using a broader term than "captured" which was used in the Geneva P.O.W. Convention of 1929.[191] It was sometimes contended during the Second World War that where regulars surrendered in mass they had not been "captured" and consequently it was not legally required to accord them P.O.W. status.

The introductory wording of article 4A(2) concerning irregulars goes beyond article 1 of the Hague Regulations. It characterizes privileged combatants who do not comprise a part of the regular armed forces as members of "other militias and members of other volunteer corps, including those of organized resistance movements." The inclusion of "organized resistance movements" is based upon the experience of the Second World War and accords authority and status for such movements which are similar or analogous to the wartime model.[192] The broad language which is made applicable to these resistance movements, "operating in or outside their own territory, even if this territory is occupied," provides a comprehensive geographical area of operations for such movements which was not included in the Hague Regulations.

---

188. J. Pictet (ed.), *Commentary on the Geneva Prisoners of War Convention of 1949,* 53 (Int'l Comm. of the Red Cross, 1960) [Hereafter cited as *I.C.R.C. Commentary.* It consists of 4 volumes with one for each Convention.]

189. 2A *Final Record of the Diplomatic Conference of Geneva of 1949,* 414 (Swiss Fed. Pol. Dept., undated) [The *Final Record* comprises 4 volumes numbered 1, 2A, 2B and 3 and is cited hereafter as *Geneva Rec.*].

190. The Report of Committee II to the Plenary Assembly of the Conference. 2A *Geneva Rec.* 559, at 561-62.

191. *Supra* note 186, art. 1.

192. The Report of Committee II to the Diplomatic Conference stated that the problem of organized resistance movements was solved by assimilating them to militias and corps of volunteers not "forming part of the armed forces" of a state party to the conflict as specified in article 4A(1). This resulted in placing them in article 4A(2). 2A *Geneva Rec.* 559 at 562. The Committee concluded: "There is therefore an important innovation involved which has become necessary as a result of the experience of the Second World War." *Id.*

a. *The Requirement of Organization*

The requirement of membership in an "organized" resistance movement is explicit in the first traditional provision concerning a responsible military commander and is implicit in the other three. Its inclusion in additional wording which introduces the other provisions should be interpreted as indicating a special emphasis on the principle that irregulars or partisans should be organized in belligerent groups which better facilitate their compliance with the other conditions of the article. This basic principle had been accepted prior to the Diplomatic Conference in the agreement of the Conference of Government Experts "that the first condition preliminary to granting prisoners-of-war status to partisans was their forming a body having a military organization."[193]

The substantive requirement that resistance movements be "organized" is met by the most rudimentary elements of a military organization. Thus, a corporal's squad on detached duty meets the requirement. In the same way, a few irregulars who were part of a larger military unit broken through the exigencies of combat will qualify. A single individual separated from his organized unit retains his status as a member of the organized body even though he is unable to rejoin any part of that body before he is captured.

b. *The Requirement of "Belonging to a Party to the Conflict"*

The clearest feature of the requirement of "belonging" in article 4A(2) is that it does not mean subordination to state control because if it did, it would merely repeat the terms of article 4A(1) concerning irregulars which are part of regular armed forces. Article 4A(1) repeats the protection afforded under article 1 of the Hague Regulations for such irregulars including, for example, the Allied "commandos" of World War II. Their "belonging" to a state party to the conflict in this sense is clear.

The relationship of the irregular forces under article 4A(2) is more complicated. The I.C.R.C. *Commentary* states:

> It is essential that there should be a *de facto* relationship between the resistance organization and the party to international law which is in a state of war, but the existence of this relationship is sufficient. It may find expression merely by tacit agreement, if the operations are such as to indicate clearly for which side the resistance organization is fighting.[194]

The reference to "the party to international law" is to a subject of international law which has status as a state or an authority (public body), and this requirement of "belonging," meaning association, may be met by a loose relationship with either. An example of such an association is the French Forces of the Interior and their relationship with the Free French authority prior to July 15, 1944, at which time they came under the command of Allied regular armies under General Eisenhower.[195] They were protected by article 1 of the Hague Regulations as irregulars both while acting without state authorization and later when they were associated with the Allied armies. If the present P.O.W. Convention had been applicable, the French Forces of the Interior would have come under article 4A(2) until July 15, 1944 and after that time they would have come under 4A(1).

The term "a Party to the conflict," which is somewhat ambiguous standing alone, may be better understood by reference to the context in which it is used. It

---

193. 3 *I.C.R.C. Commentary* 58.
194. *Id.* at 57.
195. *Id.*

appears in other articles of the P.O.W. Convention in contexts in which, in order to effectuate the purposes of the Convention, it includes authorities such as the stated "organized resistance movements." The term "High Contracting Parties" which appears in articles 1 through 3 does not appear in article 4. It is used once in the common article 1 and twice in the common article 2 to refer to the state parties to the Convention. It is used in the same way at the beginning of the common article 3 concerning internal conflicts or civil wars. At the outset of that article, a different phrase, "Party to the conflict," is used to refer to all of the parties to the internal conflict. In addition to the legitimate government, this must necessarily include the revolutionaries whose military forces are typically organized as irregular groups. In some internal conflicts a revolutionary group may have a regular army structure, such as the Confederate States Army in the Civil War in the United States. In others this may not be the case. The last paragraph of article 3 uses "the Parties to the conflict" to refer to all such parties in a factual sense by providing that the application of the humanitarian provisions shall not affect their legal status. Since the legal status of states is usually not in dispute, this must refer to the status of revolutionary parties.

The next use of "a Party to the conflict" is in article 4A(1). Since this subsection deals with regular armed forces, the context which is thus provided indicates that the term here refers, at least as the norm, to state parties to the conflict. It refers to recognized state parties because subsection 4A(3) deals with regular forces of an unrecognized government or public authority. The term "a Party to the conflict" again appears in article 4A(2) in which the factual reference is to the irregular movements as parties to the conflict by linking them to operations "in or outside their own territory, even if this territory is occupied." This interpretation of the movement as a party is supported by the experience of the Second World War upon which article 4A(2) is based. Marshal Tito's Yugoslav partisan forces had allegiance to their own organized resistance movement which was a party to international law and to the international conflict.[196] They were not associated with any state party to the conflict until their successes against the German Army made it militarily advantageous to the Allied powers to develop a relationship with them. They not only rejected any suggestion of relationship with the Royal Government of Yugoslavia in exile, but were at the end of the war the creators of the contemporary Socialist Federal Republic of Yugoslavia.

Article 4A(3) of the P.O.W. Convention includes as privileged combatants:

> Members of regular armed forces who profess allegiance to a government or an authority not recognized by the Detaining Power.

This provision must be interpreted "in the light of the actual case which motivated its drafting," that of the regular armed forces of General DeGaulle "which were under the authority of the French National Liberation Committee."[197] After 1940, they continued armed struggle against Germany contrary to the terms of the Vichy French-German Armistice agreement of that year. That armistice expressly provided that French nationals who continued to bear arms against the German forces would not be considered as privileged combatants who were entitled to the protection of the laws of war. The German Government, however, subsequently acknowledged the privileged status of these forces and regarded them as "fighting for England."[198] Even if General DeGaulle's forces did not "profess allegiance"

---

196. *Supra* note 167 at 54.
197. 3 *I.C.R.C. Commentary* 62.
198. *Id.* at 63.

Three Palestinian women (above), two of them holding handkerchiefs to their faces because of the stench of death, shown on Sept. 19 passing the body of a Palestinian killed during the massacre of hundreds of men, women and children in the Sabra and Shatila refugee camps in West Beirut. Women (below) seek the bodies of relatives as Red Cross workers, civil defense volunteers and boy scouts bring the bodies of massacre victims out of the rubble of the Sabra refugee camp on Sept. 21.

to a government (they expressly opposed the Vichy French Government), the Free French constituted a public authority (not a government in exile), to which they professed allegiance, recognized by many states but not by Germany. An analagous situtation today would entitle such combatants to the same privileged treatment as P.O.W.s as other regulars. Thus article 4A(3) requires a relationship between regular armed forces and a public body party to the conflict as an alternative to that with a state party set forth in article 4A(1). The relationship requirement for irregular forces set forth in article 4A(2) is clearly not intended to be more demanding than that for regulars in 4A(3).

At the 1949 Diplomatic Conference in Geneva, the views of those who wished to impose additional requirements upon irregulars were rejected.[199] The basic criteria for irregulars remained the same as that in article 9 of the Brussels Declaration and article 1 of the Hague Regulations of 1899 and 1907, neither of which required state authorization or subjection to orders from regular army headquarters. The original Russian Government's draft of article 9 at Brussels had provided that irregulars must be subject to orders from regular army headquarters, but this provision was widely opposed and omitted in the final text. The most recent edition of *Oppenheim's International Law* by Professor Lauterpacht provides a succinct summary of the change in legal status of irregular forces before and after the Franco-Prussian War of 1870:

> Very often the armed forces of belligerents consist throughout the war of their regular armies only; but it happens frequently that irregular forces take part. Of such irregular forces two different kinds are to be distinguished—first, such as are authorised by the belligerents; and secondly, such as are acting on their own initiative, and on their own account, without special authorisation. Formerly, it was a recognised rule of International Law that only the members of authorised irregular forces enjoy the privileges due to the members of the armed forces of belligerents; . . . . But according to Article 1 of the Hague Regulations this rule is now obsolete. Its place is taken by the rule that irregulars enjoy the privileges due to members of the armed forces of the belligerents, although they do not act under authorisation. . . .[200]

Article 4A(2) increased the preexisting category of irregulars by specifically including "organized resistance movements" based on the experience of the Second World War. The interpretation of "a Party to the conflict" which is consistent with the Brussels and Hague criteria is that it makes a broad factual reference under which the organized resistance movement may be its own party to the conflict. This interpretation also makes the word "belonging" in the English text more accurate because organized resistance forces can clearly "belong" to their own movement which is a party to the conflict.[201] Such forces cannot "belong," in the sense of subordination and control, to a state party to the conflict and remain under the protection of article 4A(2). If state control existed, the protection would be afforded by article 4A(1).

c. *The Requirement of Responsible Military Command*

This provision and the ensuing three are the same traditional requirments of article 9 of the Brussels Declaration and article 1 of the Hague Regulations. The requirement limits privileged status to those irregulars who are a part of a belligerent group with a command structure which has responsibility for the actions of its

---

199. *Supra* note 190 at 562.
200. 2 *Oppenheim's International Law* 256-57 (7th ed., Lauterpacht, 1952).
201. The equally authoritative French text of art. 4A(2) uses the somewhat less specific word, "appartenant."

members. It is not necessary that a commander be a regular army officer or be commissioned by a government. The U.S. Army Manual, *The Law of Land Warfare*, declares that "State recognition, however, is not essential and an organization may be formed spontaneously and elect its own officers."[202] The main purpose for having a "responsible commander" is to provide for reasonable assurance of adherence by irregulars to the fundamental requirement of compliance with the laws of war. It is thought that a somewhat effective sanction exists by making the commander "responsible for his subordinates." Although there is no stated limitation upon the responsibility of the commander, the requirement should be interpreted so as to effectuate its major purpose. While the dividing line cannot be fixed in advance so as to cover all possible fact situations, some of the clearer ones can be identified. If subordinates attack noncombatant targets in a military operation, the commander is responsible. If a subordinate commits an isolated murder for his own personal objectives while not subject to the control of the commander, the latter is not responsible. Command must be exercised in the preparation and execution of military operations, but not at all times without exception.

In the post World War II war crimes trials, the defense of superior orders was available to subordinates in some situations. In general, it was not treated as a bar to the conviction of a subordinate for executing an illegal order, but, dependent upon all the circumstances, it was considered in mitigation of punishment.[203] It should be apparent that unless some effect is given to the defense of superior orders, each subordinate is invited to determine the legality of orders for himself with destructive consequences for the discipline which is an inseparable part of military command. There is no doubt that the commander who issues illegal orders is responsible for them.[204]

d. *The Requirement of a Fixed Distinctive Sign*

Article 4A(2) (b) prescribes "having a fixed distinctive sign recognizable at a distance." This distinctive sign requirement for the irregular is analogous to the wearing of a uniform by a regular. The requirement is designed to allow privileged status to those combatants who are distinguishable in appearance from the civilian population. The sign must nominally be "fixed," but it is widely agreed that the requirement is met by an armband, an insignia, or, for example, a distinctive headgear or coat.[205] The requirement that the sign be "recognizable at a distance" is rather vague since there is no specification of such obvious questions as to what distance, by whom, and in what circumstances. The distinctive sign of irregulars, like the uniform of regulars, need only be worn during military operations. Such operations should be reasonably construed as including deployments which are preliminary to actual combat.

---

202. Field Manual 27-10, *The Law of Land Warfare*, p. 27, para. 64 (1956).
203. McDougal & Feliciano, *Law and Minimum World Public Order*, 690-99 (1961); Parks, "Command Responsibility for War Crimes," 62 *Mil. L. Rev.* 1 (1973).
204. *Trial of Kurt Meyer*, "The Abbaye Ardenne Case," 4 Rep. U.N. Comm. 97 (Can. Mil. Ct., Aurich, Germany, 1945); *Trial of Baba Masao*, 11 Rep. U.N. Comm. 56 (Austl. Mil. Ct., Rabaul, 1947); *Trial of Wilhelm Von Leeb*, "The German High Command Trial," 12 Rep. U.N. Comm. 1 (U.S. Mil. Trib., Nuremberg, 1948). The cited cases deal with regular army commanders but it is unlikely that a significantly different standard would be applied to irregular commanders.
205. *Supra* note 202.

e. The Requirement of Open Arms

The purpose of the requirement of "carrying arms openly," like the requirement of a distinctive sign, is to prevent irregulars, at the risk of forfeiting their privileged status as prisoners of war upon capture, perfidiously misleading the enemy by concealing their own identity.[206] The conditions of "open arms" and "distinctive sign" emphasize the necessity that irregulars distinguish themselves as combatants during their operations against the enemy. The I.C.R.C. *Commentary* states that the requirement that arms be carried "openly" means that the "enemy must be able to recognize partisans as combatants in the same way as regular armed forces, whatever their weapons."[207] Similarly, it cannot be interpreted to mean that irregulars are under an obligation to carry their arms more openly than do regular soldiers.[208] The open arms requirement, like that of the distinctive sign, is only applicable during military operations.

f. The Requirement of Compliance with Laws and Customs of War

(1) Analysis of the Requirement

This requirement is an expression of the fundamental concept which constitutes the basis for the whole body of the law of armed conflict. Unless hostilities "are to degenerate into a savage contest of physical forces freed from all restraints," the laws and customs of war must continue to be observed in all relevant circumstances.[209] This requirement prescribes that irregulars, like regulars, are bound to conform in the conduct of their operations to the recognized standards of the international humanitarian law.

While it is clear that the present requirement includes each of the preceding criteria of article 4A(2), its full ambit is not defined with precision. The I.C.R.C. *Commentary* recognizes that "the concept of the laws and customs of war is rather vague and subject to variations as the forms of war evolve."[210] In spite of the problem of "vagueness," however, there exist at least some criteria for judging the lawfulness of the particular actions of irregular combatants and for holding the perpetrators of illegitimate acts of warfare criminally responsible for their behavior. The U.S. Army, *Law of Land Warfare,* provides a representative description of such conduct considered violative of the laws and customs of war by especially warning against:

> employment of treachery, denial of quarter, maltreatment of prisoners of war, wounded and dead, improper conduct toward flags of truce, pillage, and unnecessary violence and destruction.[211]

These acts would, of course, be equally violative of law if committed by regular forces. In either case they would be punishable as war crimes as opposed to common crimes under municipal criminal law.

A further explanation of the basic character of the condition of adhering to the laws and customs of war is provided in the I.C.R.C. *Commentary*:

> Partisans [irregulars] are...required to respect the Geneva Conventions *to the fullest extent possible*. In particular, they must conform to international agreements as those which prohibit the use of certain weapons (gas). In all their operations, they must be

---

206. *Supra* note 200 at 430.
207. 3 *I.C.R.C. Commentary* 61.
208. *Id.*
209. *Supra* note 200 at 218.
210. *Supra* note 207.
211. *Supra* note 202 at p. 28, para. 64.

guided by the moral criteria which, in the absence of written provisions, must direct the conscience of man; in launching attacks, they must not cause violence and suffering disproportionate to the military result which they may reasonably hope to achieve. They may not attack civilians or disarmed persons and must, in all their operations, respect the principles of honour and loyalty *as they expect their enemies to do.*[212]

The last italicized clause of the statement implies the consequences of a belligerent state's persistent and demonstrable disregard of the rules of international law. As a practical matter in obtaining enforcement of the laws and customs of war by resistance movements "operating in or outside their own territory," observance of the doctrines by state-parties to the conflict is important in establishing conditions for mutuality and reciprocity which promote similar observance by irregulars. In addition, the state-parties to the 1949 Geneva Conventions have unilateral obligations, not contingent upon mutuality, including the common article 1 requirement "to respect and to ensure respect" for the Conventions. Since resistance movements were not, as such, represented at Geneva in 1949, it is fatuous to expect them to adhere to the laws and customs of war in situations where there are violations by the states which wrote and adopted the rules.

The humanitarian treatment of prisoners of war in contemporary conflict situations is an appropriate subject for concern. It is clear that the state-parties to the 1949 P.O.W. Convention are bound to carry out all of the very detailed administrative arrangements concerning the protection and care of P.O.W.s which appear in the one hundred forty-three articles of the Convention. It would require a considerable departure from reality to expect irregular forces to meet the same requirements in the treatment of P.O.W.s in their hands. A provision of the draft P.O.W. Convention prepared by the I.C.R.C. stated that irregulars, in addition to the four criteria first formulated in the Brussels Declaration, must also "treat nationals of the Occupying Power who fall into their hands in accordance with the provisions of the present Convention."[213] This provision was deleted by the Diplomatic Conference because of an unwillingness to impose additional criteria beyond the four traditional ones. The outcome is a recognition of the realities with which irregular forces and their P.O.W.s are confronted. One should not, however, reach the opposite conclusion and believe that prisoners are at the mercy of irregular forces. At the minimum, fundamental humanitarian treatment must be accorded to prisoners in the hands of irregulars.

It is necessary to consider briefly the applicability of each of the six criteria of article 4A(2) to the group and to its individual members. Each of the six criteria is imposed upon the irregular group as an entity. According to the widely accepted view, if the group does not meet the first three criteria (organization, association with a factual party to the conflict, either a state or a public body, and military command), the individual member cannot qualify for privileged status as a P.O.W.[214] The last three criteria (distinctive sign, open arms, and adhering to the laws and customs) must be met by most of the members of the group to entitle the individual member to privileged status.[215] The individual may not be denied P.O.W. status except by the decision of a properly qualified court which meets the criteria of the P.O.W. Convention.[216] Because of both the need to bring irregulars

---

212. *Supra* note 207. (Emphasis added.)
213. Draft art. 3(6)(b). 1 *Geneva Rec.* 73, 74.
214. *Supra* note 167 at 62.
215. See the text accompanying *infra* note 235.
216. Art. 5(2).

within the legal system and the humanitarian purpose of the applicable law, state officials may not lightly reach the conclusion that most of the members of an irregular group do not comply with the last three criteria.

(2) Situations Where Reprisals Are Applicable

The Geneva Conventions for the Protection of War Victims of 1949 have prohibited all reprisals against P.O.W.s, civilians, and militarily ineffective combatants, that is, those who are wounded, sick, or shipwrecked.[217] This leaves reprisals still applicable to effective combatant forces. The U.S. Army, *Law of Land Warfare*, provides the following definition:

> Reprisals are acts of retaliation in the form of conduct which would otherwise be unlawful, resorted to by one belligerent against enemy personnel or property for acts of warfare committed by the other belligerent in violation of the law of war, for the purpose of enforcing future compliance with the recognized rules of civilized warfare.[218]

Reprisals may be lawfully invoked, *inter alia*, where irregular or regular armed forces are responding to prior violations of the laws and customs of war by the opposing belligerent.[219]

2. Application of the Law Concerning P.O.W.s to the Fact Situation in Lebanon

a. Denial of P.O.W. Status

On July 18, 1982 the Government of Israel Ministry of Foreign Affairs conducted a briefing and distributed a statement entitled "The Israeli Operation in Lebanon: Legal Aspects." It stated, *inter alia*:

> From the outset of the operation, Israel declared to the International Committee of the Red Cross, that it will apply, as appropriate, the four Geneva Conventions. Accordingly, both during and since the hostilities, Israel has duly applied those conventions.[220]

Another portion of the statement involved the according of prisoner of war status. It stated that Syrian Army regulars would be given such status.[221] No mention was made of Lebanese Army regulars or Lebanese militias. The statement also made no specific mention of Palestinian regular forces such as those comprising the Palestine Liberation Army.[222] It denies P.O.W. status to all Palestinian forces by providing:

---

217. Conv. I: art. 46; Conv. II: art. 47; Conv. III: art. 13(3); Conv. IV: art. 33(3). The four Conventions are cited fully in *supra* notes 180-182.
218. *Supra* note 202 at p. 177, para. 498(a). The same source in para. 497(b) stresses that reprisals should not be resorted to in a hasty and ill-considered manner. See, F. Kalshoven, *Belligerent Reprisals, passim* (1971).
219. *Re Christiansen,* [1948] An. Dig. Int'l L. Cases 412 at 413 (Netherlands Special Court, War Criminals, 1948).
220. Israel Ministry of Foreign Affairs, Information Division, Briefing No. 342 at p. 4.
221. *Id.*
222. The Palestine Liberation Army, which consists of regular troops, operates under the authority of the P.L.O. Executive Committee. See the organization chart in H. Sharabi, *Palestine Guerrillas: Their Credibility and Effectiveness* 45 (Georgetown, 1970).

The PLO and its associated terror groups do not fall within any of the categories formulated in the Convention regarding persons entitled to the status of prisoners-of-war. They are not "regular armed forces" and do not constitute an "organized resistance movement belonging to a party to the conflict" (Article 4A).[223]

Reports in the press confirm this decision of the Government of Israel not to accord the privileged status to captured Palestinian combatants. For example, an article by William Claiborne printed in the Washington Post as early as June 13, 1982 quoted an Israeli Army command source as stating: "They are terrorists. We don't refer to them as prisoners-of-war."[224] The same source then was stated to have listed the four traditional Brussels-Hague-Geneva criteria applicable to irregulars entitled to P.O.W. status, and the Claiborne article continued:

> While some of the criteria may be arguable, a military source said, the guerrillas clearly have not conducted their operations in accordance with the laws and customs of war.[225]

Also, according to the same article:

> Although Army officials declined to acknowledge it, refusal to grant internationally recognized prisoner-of-war status to the guerrillas apparently is the result of a political decision stemming from a reluctance of Israeli officials to recognize the Palestine Liberation Organization as a legitimate armed force.[226]

Another indication of the Government of Israel's juridical position was reported in an article by James Feron in the New York Times of August 26, 1982.[227] This article states that in the negotiations which led to the PLO departure from Beirut, Israel demanded that the PLO release Israeli P.O.W.s which it was holding,[228] but there was no comparable agreement requiring the release of Palestinian combatants captured by the Israeli Army.[229] The reason given for this by an Israeli Government official was that Israel had rejected the concept of reciprocity because the Palestinians were holding soldiers while the Israelis were holding civilians.[230] The following analysis was attributed by Mr. Feron to Mr.

---

223. *Supra* note 220. This characterization is not consistent, however, with some Israeli statements. For example:

> Sharon [Israeli Defense Minister] said military intelligence experts were "astounded" to discover the extent of the P.L.O. conventional military apparatus in eastern Lebanon. He said that in the territory covered by the Israeli Army, the Palestinians had 15,000 to 20,000 regular troops and 40,000 irregulars.

Wash. Post, June 12, 1982, p. A1, col. 6, cont. p. A20, cols. 5-6, at col. 6. The former chief of military intelligence, Aharon Yariv, stated that "Fatah had units organized in battalions and brigades." Jerusalem Post Int'l Ed., Oct. 3-9, 1982, p. 15, cols. 1-5, at col. 1.
224. Wash. Post, June 13, 1982, p. A25, cols. 1-3, at col. 1.
225. *Id.* at col. 3.
226. *Id.* at cols. 2-3.
227. New York Times, Aug. 26, 1982, p. A1, col. 1, cont. p. A14, cols. 1-6.
228. *Id.* at p. A14, col. 4.
229. *Id.* These statements are consistent with the ultimate agreement entitled, Plan for the Departure from Lebanon of the PLO Leadership, Offices, and Combatants in Beirut, art. 21 (Aug. 19, 1982). On Aug. 20, President Reagan announced the assent of Lebanon, The United States, France, Italy, Israel and the P.L.O. to this agreement. The agreement and a portion of its context is in U.S. Dept. State, Bureau of Public Affairs, *Lebanon: Plan for the PLO Evacuation From West Beirut* (Current Policy Pub. No. 415, August 1982).
230. *Supra* note 227 at p. A14, col. 4.

Alan Baker, the Assistant Legal Adviser of the Israeli Foreign Ministry:

> He said that the Syrian soldiers in west Beirut, roughly a third of those trapped there in the fighting, "are entitled to the privileges of prisoners of war, but not the terrorists."[231]

Mr. Feron explained that "Israelis use the word 'terrorists' to refer to the Palestininian guerrillas."[232] The analysis then continued:

> Mr. Baker said that the third Geneva Convention did, in fact, have a category "concerning militias, but they have to belong to a party to the conflict and follow four rules: carry arms openly, operate under a fixed command, wear uniforms and follow the rules and customs of war."
>
> "The P.L.O.," he said, "does not fulfill those requirements, especially following the laws and customs of war." He cited "hijacking, taking actions against civilians and avoiding military activities" as examples.[233]

While, in the views attributed above to an Israeli military source, "some of the criteria may be arguable," the principal Israeli claim is that the Palestinian armed forces (principally irregulars) have not conducted "their operations in accordance with the laws and customs of war."[234] Such a claim must be appraised under the established law which is stated succinctly in *The Law of Land Warfare:*

> This condition [compliance with law] is fulfilled if most of the members of the body observe the laws and customs of war, notwithstanding the fact that the individual member concerned may have committed a war crime.[235]

Although in the past there have been incidents involving a small number of PLO combatants, as well as dissident Palestinian groups, in clear violation of the laws and customs of war including attacking civilians and hijacking aircraft, no credible evidence has shown that the majority of the thousands of Palestinian combatants have engaged in such conduct. If the Israeli argument that the actions of a small minority disentitles the majority to P.O.W. status were accepted, the consistent massive and continuing Israel Defense Force violations of the laws and customs of war in Lebanon as well as in actions against Palestinians in the other occupied territories would likewise disentitle every captured Israeli soldier to P.O.W. status.[236] The PLO, nevertheless, has accorded this privileged status to Israelis captured in Lebanon.[237]

No Israeli statement of intention concerning denial of P.O.W. status to Lebanese irregulars fighting on the same side as the Palestinian irregulars is known to exist. However, the media reports of treatment accorded to all irregulars by Israel does not suggest any distinction between Lebanese and Palestinians.[238]

---

231. *Id.*
232. *Id.*
233. *Id.* Mr. Baker's words quoted in the first paragraph indicate confusion concerning military command and "fixed distinctive sign" (not a uniform).
234. *Supra* note 224, p. A25, at col. 3.
235. *Supra* note 202, at p. 28, para. 64.
236. Further examples of the evidence concerning Israeli violations are considered in the remainder of this study.
237. An article by Mr. Loren Jenkins headlined, "PLO Demands Israel Supply List of its Prisoners" reported eight Israeli P.O.W.s being held by the PLO, Wash. Post, Sept. 9, 1982, p. A29, cols. 2-5. Thus far there has been no list of Palestinian P.O.W.s supplied to the P.L.O.
238. *E.g.,* Wash. Post, July 28, 1982, p. A1, cols. 2-4 cont. p. A16, cols. 3-5.

Lebanese irregulars are, of course, entitled to P.O.W. status upon the same criteria applicable to other irregulars under article 4A(2).

Article 4A(6) of the P.O.W. Convention expressly provides P.O.W. status for civilians "who on the approach of the enemy spontaneously take up arms to resist the invading forces" and this fits the situation of those civilians, whether Lebanese or Palestinian, who attempted to resist the Israeli invasion of Lebanon. The only requirements applicable to them are that "they carry arms openly and respect the laws and customs of war." It is no more necessary for them to be under the direction and control of a state party to the conflict than it is for regulars under article 4A(3) or for irregulars under 4A(2).

The P.O.W. Convention provides specifically for the procedure to be followed concerning persons whose status is in doubt. Its article 5(2) states:

> Should any doubt arise as to whether persons, having committed a belligerent act and having fallen into the hands of the enemy, belong to any of the categories enumerated in Article 4, such persons shall enjoy the protection of the present Convention until such time as their status has been determined by a competent tribunal.

In the draft wording prepared by the International Committee of the Red Cross, the last four words read "by some responsible authority."[239] This wording was thought to be subject to abuse and therefore the 1949 Diplomatic Conference in Geneva substituted the requirement of "a competent tribunal."

Article 84(2) provides:

> In no circumstances whatever shall a prisoner of war be tried in a court of any kind which does not offer the essential guarantees of independence and impartiality as generally recognized, and, in particular, the procedure of which does not afford the accused the right and means of defence provided for in article 105.

A report by Edward Cody from "Sidon, Israeli-Occupied Lebanon" printed in the Washington Post on June 22, 1982 states:

> Israeli soldiers scouring the occupied Lebanese countryside have rounded up between 5,000 and 6,000 Palestinians and are holding them in internment camps in Lebanon and Israel.[240]
>
> * * *
>
> Eventually some may be brought to trial under an Israeli law that allows the government to prosecute PLO members—even if they joined outside Israel—as members of a hostile organization. Justice Minister Moshe Nissim has appointed two special tribunals to weigh the question.[241]

If these individuals are entitled to P.O.W. status, the conduct of such trials would be in violation of the requirements of the P.O.W. Convention. If they are civilians, any trial of them must conform to the requirments of the Civilians Convention and trial under such a statute would not do so.

In summary, the Government of Israel's denial of P.O.W. status to those entitled to it during the invasion of Lebanon is a flagrant violation of the Hague Regulations applicable in World War II, which is still recognized treaty law and which has become binding customary law. In the trial of the major German defendants before the International Military Tribunal at Nuremberg and in the subsequent war crimes trials, Germans were convicted of war crimes because of the

---

239. Draft art. 4(2), 1 *Geneva Rec.* 73 at 74.
240. Wash. Post, June 22, 1982, p. A14, cols. 1-4, at col. 1.
241. *Id.* at col. 4.

denial of P.O.W. status to partisans (irregulars) who were entitled to it under article 1 of the Hague Regulations of 1907.[242] Under the criteria of the Hague Regulations which were applied in those cases, Israeli defendants would be equally guilty of war crimes, and today convictions would be even more certain because irregular combatants now enjoy increased protection as a result of the amplified wording of article 4A(2) of the 1949 Geneva P.O.W. Convention.[243]

b. Violation of the Required Standard of Treatment of P.O.W.s and Civilian Detainees

Since the Government of Israel has made no distinction between its treatment of P.O.W.s and civilian detainees, the facts of both situations must be treated together. According to the Red Cross *Commentary* on the Civilians Convention, whatever the category of the detained persons:

> Every person in enemy hands must have some status under international law: he is either a prisoner of war and as such, covered by the Third Convention, a civilian covered by the Fourth Convention, or again, a member of the medical personnel of the armed forces who is covered by the First Convention. *There is no* intermediate status; nobody in enemy hands can be outside the law.[244]

Articles 12 to 15 of the P.O.W. Convention provide the basic criteria which must be followed in the protection of P.O.W.s. Article 12 provides, *inter alia,* that P.O.W.s are in the care of the capturing government and states that, "Irrespective of the individual responsibilities that may exist, the Detaining Power is responsible for the treatment given them."[245] Article 13 expressly prohibits reprisals against P.O.W.s and provides, *inter alia:*

> Prisoners of war must at all times be humanely treated. Any unlawful act or omission by the Detaining Power causing death or seriously endangering the health of a prisoner of war in its custody is prohibited and will be regarded as a serious breach of the present Convention.[246]

Article 14 requires respect in all circumstances for the persons and the honor of prisoners and includes special protection for women. Article 15 provides for necessary medical attention and this means, at the least, the standard of medical care usually provided in the captor's armed forces. These standards apply to the protection of P.O.W.s in the hands of irregulars as well as regular forces, as a part of the obligation of the parties to the conflict to obey the laws and customs of war. Articles 27 through 34 of the Civilians Convention provide analagous protections for civilians.

---

242. *E.g.,* the conviction of Field Marshall Keitel. 1 I.M.T. 171 at 289-91; *Trial of Carl Bauer,* 8 Rep. U.N. Comm. 15, (Permanent Mil. Tribunal, Dijon, 1945).
243. In *Military Prosecutor v. Kassem,* 42 Int'l L. Rep. 470 (Israeli Military Court, Ramallah, 1969), Palestinian irregulars were denied P.O.W. status and convicted under Israeli municipal law. The case is criticized in *supra* note 167 at 71-72 and by Professor Georg Schwarzenberger in "Human Rights and Guerrilla Warfare," 1 *Israel Y.B. Human Rts.* 246, 249-50 (1951) who points out that the Israeli court did not adhere to the interpretive principle requiring humanitarian conventions to be liberally interpreted to achieve their protective purposes.
244. 4 *I.C.R.C. Commentary* 51. The same source points out that irregulars who do not meet the criteria of art. 4A(2) of the P.O.W. Convention are protected persons under the Civilians Convention. *Id.* at 50.
245. Art. 12(1).
246. Art. 13(1).

Jonathan C. Randal stated in an article in the Washington Post on July 28, 1982:

> For more than a month after Israel began taking prisoners in Lebanon, it declined to authorize customary prison visits by the International Committee of the Red Cross, causing the ICRC to set aside its traditional discretion and to drop public hints indicating its displeasure. The Israelis later yielded and the visits were allowed.[247]

It was pointed out that the ICRC representative was permitted into Ansar prison camp beginning on July 18 and that on July 22, "for the first time in its association with the Arab-Israeli conflict stretching back to the late 1940s," the ICRC took the initiative to interrupt the visits.[248] In keeping with the tradition of public discretion, no reason was stated for the interruption. The visits were resumed on July 26 after a more satisfactory arrangement had apparently been made.[249]

Mr. William Claiborne reported in the Washington Post on June 13, 1982 that: "Israeli Army trucks filled with handcuffed and blindfolded prisoners have been seen leaving Lebanon for undisclosed sites in Israel."[250] Numerous other press reports stated the same essential facts.[251] There have been no press reports concerning treatment accorded to the prisoners upon their arrival at the "undisclosed sites in Israel," but the facts that are known from the accounts of a few individuals who have been released show that the treatment falls far below the required standard.

Dr. Chris Giannou, a Canadian surgeon serving with the Palestine Red Crescent Society (P.R.C.S.) in Lebanon, provided some of the relevant facts in testimony presented to the Subcommittee on Europe and the Middle East of the U.S. House of Representatives Committee on Foreign Affairs on July 13, 1982.[252] He was serving as Medical Director of the Nabatieh Hospital and was temporarily working in Sidon, Lebanon at the time of the Israeli invasion. He testified, *inter alia,* that the entire male population of Sidon "which had crossed Israeli lines to

---

247. *Supra* note 238 at p. A1, col. 4.
248. *Id.* at p. A16, cols. 3-4. The grim conditions in Ansar, including reports of beatings and torture, and hooded informers identifying suspects in Sidon are reported by Ms. Trudy Rubin under the heading, "'What will happen to the detainees is a political question,' Israelis say." Christian Sci. Monitor, Aug. 5, 1982, p. 12, cols. 1-4, cont. p. 13, col. 1. One Israeli official was quoted concerning the prisoners: "They are 100 percent terrorists." *Id.* at p. 12, col. 1.
249. *Supra* note 238 at p. A16, col. 4.
250. *Supra* note 224 at p. A25, col. 3.
251. *E.g.,* New York Times, Aug. 27, 1982, p. A14, cols. 4-6, at col. 5; The Guardian (London), Sept. 7, 1982, p. 6, col. 1; Christian Sci. Monitor, Aug. 5, 1982, p. 12, cols. 1-4 at col. 3:

    > Israel permits no access to Palestinians detained in Israel. (United Nations peacekeeping forces stationed near Tyre report still seeing busloads of blindfolded prisoners moving south to Israel.)

252. *United States Policy Toward Lebanon—Relief and Rehabilitation Assistance,* Hearings Before the Committee on Foreign Affairs and the Subcommittee on Europe and the Middle East, 97th Cong., 2nd Sess. 106-113 (1982).

    Dr. Giannou also testified before the "International Commission to Enquire into Reported Violations of International Law by Israel During its Invasion of the Lebanon" chaired by Sean MacBride and composed of Professor Richard Falk, Dean Kader Asmal, Dr. Brian Bercusson, Professor Geraud de la Pradelle, and Professor Stefan Wild. *Israel in Lebanon: The Report of the International Commission,* 239-41 (London, 1983) (hereafter cited as *MacBride Comm.*).

get out of the zone of hostilities" was paraded by the Israeli Army past hooded informers, and those who were denounced had a marking placed on their back.[253] In this way between 4,000 and 5,000 men were arrested including Dr. Giannou, "two Norwegian colleagues, and the entire male medical staff of the PRCS in Sidon."[254] Dr. Giannou was detained in Sidon from June 13 to June 16 and then, until his release on June 20, he was detained in the Megiddo (Armageddon) Prison in the north of Israel. He stated that in Sidon 500 to 600 prisoners were confined at one time in a convent schoolyard under difficult conditions including hands being bound, stifling heat, and food and water in short supply. He saw and heard "savage and indiscriminate beatings of the prisoners by the forty Israeli guards";[255] and he stated that a prisoner who called out for water would be subject to particular physical violence. Dr. Giannou pointed out that he and two other Europeans (the Norwegian members of the P.R.C.S. medical facility) were not beaten but that the "darker-skinned Arabs, Africans, and Asians" were beaten most severely.[256] This is a flagrant violation of article 16 of the P.O.W. Convention which is a reaction to the discriminatory practices of the Nazis. It prohibits adverse distinctions "based on race, nationality, religious beliefs or political opinions, or any other distinction founded on similar criteria." He also recounts being a witness to prisoners being beaten to death.[257] Some of these events took place in the presence of the Israeli military governor of Sidon, Colonel Arnon Amozer, and other Israeli Army officers.[258] He indicated that some Israeli guards did attempt to stop the beatings but were unsuccessful.

Dr. Giannou's testimony was corroborated by his two Norwegian colleagues who worked with the P.R.C.S., Dr. Steinar Berge and Mr. Oyind Moller. They were with Dr. Giannou in the schoolyard in Sidon and a report of their experiences, translated by the Norwegian Foreign Ministry, was distributed by them during their visit to the United States. The Canadian and Norwegian Embassies in Washington refuted the claim made by the Israeli Embassy that their respective nationals were held because they were connected with European terrorist organizations.[259]

Articles 129 and 130 of the P.O.W. Convention are similar to the corresponding articles concerning grave breaches of the Civilians Convention.[260] Article 129 provides that the parties to the Convention agree to enact necessary domestic legislation "to provide effective penal sanctions for persons committing, or ordering to be committed, any of the grave breaches of the present convention defined

253. *House Foreign Affairs Hearings, supra* note 252 at 110.
254. *Id.*
255. *Id.* at 111.
256. *Id.* at 112.
257. *Id.*
258. *Id.*
259. The official statement of the Norwegian Embassy issued to the press on July 21, 1982, read:

> The Royal Norwegian Embassy hereby confirms that Dr. Steinar Berge and Mr. Oyind Moller were working as *bona fide* health workers in full agreement with the Lebanese Government at the time when they were arrested by Israeli officials. No explanation for their detention has been given by Israeli authorities. The Norwegian Government categorically rejects the accusations made by the Israeli Embassy in Washington, D.C. to the effect that the two Norwegian citizens should have connections to European terrorist organizations.

The analagous Canadian statement appears in House Foreign Affairs Hearings, *supra* note 252, at 321.
260. Arts. 146 and 147 of the Civilians Convention.

in the following Article."[261] It also provides that the parties are obligated to search for and to bring to trial persons suspected of committing such grave breaches.[262] Article 130 provides in full:

> Grave breaches to which the preceding Article relates shall be those involving any of the following acts, if committed against persons or property protected by the Convention: wilful killing, torture or inhuman treatment including biological experiments, wilfully causing great suffering or serious injury to body or health, compelling a prisoner of war to serve in the forces of the hostile Power, or wilfully depriving a prisoner of war of the rights of fair and regular trial prescribed in this Convention.

The facts recounted by Dr. Giannou, Dr. Berge, and Mr. Moller indicate that officers and other members of the Israeli armed forces have committed the grave breaches specified in article 130 by carrying out acts, *inter alia*, of "wilful killing, torture, or inhuman treatment." These acts constitute war crimes when committed against those entitled to P.O.W. status and crimes against humanity when committed against civilian persons.[263] In addition to the individual responsibility of those persons carrying out the acts and those who ordered them, the Government of Israel is itself responsible under general principles of international law[264] as well as under article 131 of the P.O.W. Convention and article 148 of the Civilians Convention. The "grave breaches" articles of the Conventions are designed to deter inhumane treatment of the kind that has taken place in Lebanon and Israel. If deterrence is not successful, the secondary purpose is to provide punishment for those who are responsible.

C. The Geneva Conventions Concerning the Protection of Wounded and Sick Combatants and of Civilian Persons and Objects

1. The Scope of Protections Under the Conventions

The conflict situation in Lebanon has involved matters which come under the protections of both the Geneva Convention for the Amelioration of the Condition of the Wounded and Sick in Armed Forces in the Field (Convention I, known as the "Land Warfare Convention")[265] and the Convention Relative to the Protection of Civilian Persons in Time of War (Convention IV, known as the "Civilians Convention")[266] of August 12, 1949. In particular, the protections afforded to wounded and sick combatants and civilians and to the medical personnel and facilities involved in their care must be considered together because both types of wounded and sick have been treated without distinction in the limited medical facilities which were available. The special protections for civilian persons and civilian objects, of course, come under the law of the Civilians Convention.

It is of particular significance that the common article 2 of all four Geneva Conventions of 1949 was designed to make each Convention applicable broadly

---

261. Art. 146(1).
262. Art. 146(2).
263. *Judgment,* 1 I.M.T. 171 at 226-38.
264. *E.g.,* I. Brownlie, *Principles of Public International Law, passim* and Chap. 18 entitled, "The Responsibility of States" (1966).
265. 75 U.N.T.S. 31; Schindler & Toman, *supra* note 171, at 305.
266. 75 U.N.T.S. 287; Schindler & Toman, *supra* note 171, at 427.

to international conflict situations. The first paragraph in article 2 provides in part:

> [T]he present Convention shall apply to all cases of declared war or of any other armed conflict which may arise between two or more of the High Contracting Parties, even if the state of war is not recognized by one of them.

This new provision goes beyond the historically well-established situation of "all cases of declared war" and encompasses "any other armed conflict" which may arise between the parties "even if the state of war is not recognized by one of them." The change brought about by this carefully considered provision is that these Conventions apply to the facts of international armed conflict and are in no way dependent on the existence of a supposed technical "state of war."

The second paragraph of article 2 prescribes:

> The Convention shall also apply to all cases of partial or total occupation of the territory of a High Contracting Party, even if the said occupation meets with no armed resistance.

Thus the former requirement of a militarily effective occupation found in Hague Conventions II (1899)[267] and IV (1907)[268] as a prerequisite to the application of the legal protections has been eliminated and this results in more comprehensive application of each of the Conventions. There is no longer a distinction between the invasion phase and the establishment of a belligerent occupation regime as there was under the Hague law. The I.C.R.C. *Commentary* on the Civilians Convention states:

> Even a patrol which penetrated into enemy territory without any intention of staying there must respect the Convention in its dealings with the civilians it meets.[269]

One of the principal purposes of the humanitarian law is to protect noncombatants (civilians) as well as disabled combatants from the more destructive consequences of armed conflict. Civilians are usually defined as individuals who are not members of the armed forces and who do not participate in military operations. Civilians who need protection in international conflict situations fall into two categories: those who are living in territory which, while not under the control of an enemy, is subject to attack by an enemy state, and those who are living under belligerent occupation. The Civilians Convention of 1949 affords protections to both categories.

The distinction between the civilian population and combatants which began with Grotius and was reflected in Lieber's Code was further advanced in the unratified Brussels Declaration.[270] Provisions of Hague Conventions II (1899) and IV (1907), like the Brussels Declaration, contain the prohibition against forcing the inhabitants of occupied territory to take any part in military operations against their own country or to swear allegiance to the hostile power, as well as the provisions concerning the protection of family honor and rights, lives and property, and religious convictions and practices. They also have provisions forbidding pillage and collective penalties. The Geneva Civilians Convention of 1949 sets forth much more detailed provisions for the protection of noncombatants.

---

267. *Supra* note 174.
268. *Supra* note 175.
269. 4 *I.C.R.C. Commentary* 60.
270. Schindler & Toman, *supra* note 171, at 25.

The Geneva Convention for the Amelioration of the Condition of the Wounded in Armies in the Field of 22 August 1864[271] was the first multilateral treaty which provided protection for wounded military personnel as well as for military hospitals and their personnel. Later Geneva Conventions of 6 July 1906 and 27 July 1929[272] provided more detailed rules. The presently effective standards for the protection of medical facilities and personnel for combatants are in the Geneva Land Warfare Convention of 1949. Article 12 (1) of this Convention prescribes comprehensive protection for wounded and sick military personnel who must "be protected and respected in all circumstances." Article 13 states: "The present Convention shall apply to the wounded and sick belonging to the following categories" and it then sets forth in identical words the six subdivisions of article 4A of the P.O.W. Convention. The consequence is that Convention I applies, *inter alia,* to the wounded and sick of regular armed forces of both recognized government (subdivision 1) and unrecognized government or authority (subdivision 3) parties to the conflict and to irregular armed forces including those of an organized resistance movement which is a party to the conflict (subdivision 2), and to wounded and sick inhabitants of a non-occupied territory who, "on the approach of the enemy, spontaneously take up arms to resist the invading forces" (subdivision 6).

2. Protection of Wounded and Sick Combatants and of Civilians and Medical Personnel and Facilities

Article 19(1) of Convention I provides:

> Fixed establishments and mobile medical units of the Medical Service may in no circumstances be attacked, but shall at all times be respected and protected by the Parties to the conflict. Should they fall into the hands of the adverse Party, their personnel shall be free to pursue their duties, as long as the capturing Power has not itself ensured the necessary care of the wounded and sick found in such establishments and units.

Article 24 restates the principle that military medical personnel (as well as chaplains) "shall be respected and protected in all circumstances." There are correlative provisions for the protection of wounded and sick civilians and for their medical facilities and personnel which are found in articles 13 through 26 of Convention IV. Its article 13 specifically states the breadth of coverage of these articles to be "the whole of the populations of the countries in conflict." Article 20(1) provides:

> Persons regularly and solely engaged in the operation and administration of the civilian hospitals, including the personnel engaged in the search for, removal and transporting of and caring for wounded and sick civilians, the infirm and maternity cases, shall be respected and protected.

Since Palestine Red Crescent Society (P.R.C.S.) facilities in Lebanon were used to care for both combatants and civilians, they were protected under both the Land Warfare and the Civilians Conventions. P.R.C.S. medical personnel are protected by article 24 of the Land Warfare Convention if they are regarded as military

---

271. *Id.* at 213.
272. Both of these Conventions are entitled "Convention for the Amelioration of the Condition of the Wounded and Sick in Armies in the Field." The 1906 Convention is in *id.* at 213; the 1929 Convention is in *id.* at 257.

medical personnel and by article 20(1) of the Civilians Convention if they are classified as civilian medical personnel. As medical personnel, they must come under the protection of one of these two Conventions.

Dr. Giannou, who has been quoted previously, testified:

> I have been a witness to the entire male staff of the PRCS medical team in Sidon and Nabatieh being taken into custody, prevented from continuing their medical duties and being treated as ordinary prisoners without any respect to their person. The PRCS, once one of the main institutions for medical services in South Lebanon with 3 hospitals, numerous out-patient clinics and a center for mentally retarded children, and occupational rehabilitation...no longer exists there.[273]

In the same testimony, specific reference was made to the treatment of P.R.C.S. medical personnel:

> One Palestinian, Dr. Nabil, was at one point hung by his hands from a tree and beaten. An Iraqi surgeon, Dr. Mohammed Ibrahim, was beaten by several guards viciously, and left to lie in the sun with his face buried in the sand. Other surgeons and doctors were also beaten: Dr. Ahmed Soubra, a Lebanese; Drs. Saifeddin, Mohammad Iman and Shafiq El-Islam, Bangladeshi nationals.[274]

The report of a French commission of lawyers[275] who went to Lebanon to investigate the situation contained this statement, among others, about medical personnel:

> The Commission has been told that the Israeli Army, at Tyre and Sidon, broke into banks, confiscated account records and tracked down individuals who had been paid salaries from the PLO accounts. This applied particularly to nurses and workers employed in Palestinian hospitals. According to several witnesses, these interrogations were particularly brutal.[276]

The immunity of both civilian and military hospitals from direct attack is a specific application of the prohibition of direct attack on noncombatants which is firmly established in customary law. The protection of hospitals, however, is regarded as so important that particular provision is made for them. Analogous protection to that of article 19(1) of the Land Warfare Convention is provided by article 18(1) of the Civilians Convention which states:

> Civilian hospitals organized to give care to the wounded and sick, the infirm and maternity cases, may in no circumstances be the object of attack, but shall at all times be respected and protected by the Parties to the conflict.

According to one physician at Barbir Hospital, "every hospital in Beirut has been shelled."[277] There are specific reports concerning attacks on Acre Hospital, Gaza

273. House Foreign Affairs Hearings, *supra* note 252, at 109-110.
274. *Id.* at 111-12.
275. Report on the mission carried out in Israel 18-25 July 1982 at the request of the Center for Information on the Status of Palestinian and Lebanese Prisoners, Displaced and Missing Persons, Paris, France. The mission consisted of Dr. Geraud de la Pradelle (Professor of Law, Univ. of Paris) and four others. [Translation from the French by Ms. Anne Richardson, law student at George Washington University.]
276. *Id.* at 2.
277. New York Times, Aug. 13, 1982, p. 4, col. 6.

Hospital, Barbir Hospital and the Islamic Asylum, Triumph Hospital, and the American University Hospital.[278]

Ms. Robin Wright reported in the Sunday Times (London) under the heading "The Horror Shelling of a Defenseless Hospital," the continuing Israeli attacks upon the Dar al Ajaza Ismailia Hospital in West Beirut.[279] The article states that the patients in the hospital "are a mixture of senile geriatric patients, mentally retarded adults, and children with mental problems."[280] Hospital officials stated that more than 800 rockets and shells hit the hospital or its vicinity in one two-and-a-half hour attack.[281] A later article in the Sunday Times Magazine (London), under the heading "Beirut: Madness Heaped Upon Madness," consisted of both text and pictures concerning the same hospital.[282] The text stated, *inter alia*, that the hospital "had been established in Beirut for 30 years and was flying a red cross and a white flag from its roof."[283] After pointing out that the nearest PLO post was a half mile away, it continued: "The hospital was attacked with artillery, rocket and naval fire."[284] Another article on the same hospital in the Washington Post pointed out that most of the children suffered from advanced malnutrition and some had starved to death as a result of lack of adequate care and supplies due to the Israeli siege.[285] This Israeli action of blocking supplies essential to the care of the civilian population, including shipments by the International Committee of the Red Cross (I.C.R.C.),[286] is a violation of article 23 of the Civilians Convention which allows the free passage of medical and hospital supplies intended for civilian use.

The provisions of the Civilians Convention and of the Land Warfare Convention which have been considered indicate clearly that the states which wrote and agreed to the Conventions gave a high priority to the protection of wounded and sick individuals, whether combatants or civilians, as well as of all medical personnel and facilities. These provisions manifest an intention to go beyond the basic immunity of noncombatants by providing special protections so as to leave no doubt as to the applicable law concerning wounded and sick persons and medical personnel and facilities. The facts recounted here constitute violations of the quoted provisions of Conventions I and IV and in addition they constitute "grave breaches" under the common articles of each Convention.[287]

3. Protection of Civilians and Their Property

Articles 27 through 34 of the Civilians Convention are stated to have a broad application to the territories of the parties to the conflict as well as to occupied territories. Article 27 is one of the most fundamental provisions of the

---

278. *MacBride Comm.*, *supra* note 252, at 150; Wash. Post, June 22, 1982, p. A14, col. 1; Philadelphia Inquirer, June 30, 1982, p. 10-A, col. 1; Wash. Post, Aug. 5, 1982, p. A28, col. 2; *Time* magazine, Aug. 16, 1982, p. 10, col. 1, and p. 12, col. 3.
279. Sunday Times (London), July 4, 1982, p. 8, cols. 6-7.
280. *Id.* at col. 6.
281. *Id.* at col. 7.
282. Sunday Times Magazine (London), Aug. 15, 1982, pp. 14-19.
283. *Id.* at 15.
284. *Id.*
285. Wash. Post, Aug. 11, 1982, p. A17, cols. 1-3.
286. *E.g.,* Christian Sci. Monitor, Aug. 13, 1982, p. 13, cols. 1-4.
287. Conv. I: arts. 49-51; Conv. IV: arts. 146-149.

Convention since it establishes the principle of respect for the human person and the inviolable character of the elementary rights of individual men and women. This article provides in its first paragraph:

> Protected persons are entitled, in all circumstances to respect for their persons, their honour, their family rights, their religious convictions and practices, and their manners and customs. They shall at all times be humanely treated and shall be protected especially against all acts of violence or threats thereof and against insults and public curiosity.

The third paragraph of the same article prohibits "any adverse distinctions being made among protected persons and in particular those based on race, religion, or political opinion." This is similar to the prohibition of discriminations in article 16 of the P.O.W. Convention.

On September 18, 1982 the Washington Post carried a headline across the top of its first page which read: "Israelis Hunt Palestinian Sympathizers in Beirut: Christian Forces Join in Search."[288] The article by Mr. Loren Jenkins stated that two days after the Israeli Army drove into Moslem West Beirut, the search for Palestinian sympathizers started. It continued:

> Israel did not rely only on the tanks and troops of its regular army. Plainclothes security agents, carrying lists of suspects, led squads of soldiers through the streets in search of presumed enemies to interrogate.[289]

This selecting of victims on the prohibited basis of political opinion later led to the deployment of right-wing Christian militiamen (known locally as the "Kataeb" or Phalange) through Israeli armed forces into the Shatila and Sabra refugee camps[290] which resulted in what later became known as the massacre of Palestinian civilians.[291]

Article 27 of the Civilians Convention, along with article 16 of the P.O.W. Convention, was also violated by the racial discriminations pointed out by Dr. Giannou's testimony concerning the greater brutality of treatment accorded to darker skinned prisoners in the detention places where he was a witness.[292]

Article 29 of the Civilians Convention provides in full:

> The Party to the conflict in whose hands protected persons may be, is responsible for the treatment accorded to them by its agents, irrespective of any individual responsibility which may be incurred.

It should be mentioned that this article is not limited to the high contracting parties but makes a factual reference to all parties to the conflict, whether states, organized resistance movements, or others. This article repeats for the benefit of civilians the protection given by article 12 of the P.O.W. Convention to prisoners of war.

The Government of Israel is the party to the conflict responsible for protected persons wherever its armed forces are in belligerent occupation. It is responsible directly for its own actions or omissions, and it is also responsible for the acts of its agents as specified in article 29. In Lebanon this includes, *inter alia*,

---

288. Wash. Post, Sept. 18, 1982, p. A1, cols. 4-6, cont. p. A11, cols. 1-3.
289. *Id.* at p. A1, col. 5.
290. Wash. Post, Sept. 19, 1982, p. A1, cols. 4-6, cont. p. A18, cols. 1-2.
291. Chapter III F *infra,* entitled "The Crime of Genocide."
292. The text accompanying *supra* note 256.

responsibility for the acts of the Phalange militia and the acts of Major Haddad's *de facto* forces.[293]

Marvine Howe reported on August 18, 1982 in the New York Times, under the headline "Lebanese in Occupied South Say Israelis Give Free Rein to Lawless Militias," that "the Israelis have neutralized the very force they said they wanted to strengthen, the regular Lebanese Army."[294] Reference was made to bombing regular army barracks as well as occupying headquarters and seizing arms from Lebanese regulars.[295] There were several incidents reported of Major Haddad's *de facto* forces acting in a lawless manner including the burning and sacking of a Palestinian refugee camp which had been substantially destroyed during the Israeli attack.[296] The article also stated.

> The Israeli-backed Lebanese Christian militia of Maj. Saad Haddad today seized a kindergarten used by Palestinian and other Moslem children.[297]
> * * *
> The kindergarten had already had its troubles, receiving six direct artillery hits during the Israeli attack on the Ain Helweh camp. Later Christian militia-men of the Lebanese Phalangist Party seized the school's bus, a gift from the United Nations Children's Fund, and took much of the furniture, kitchen equipment and even toys, which had been donated by Danish and Swedish groups.[298]

Lawless acts by the Phalangist militia and by Major Haddad's *de facto* forces are not a new development. For example, the New York Times published an Associated Press account on March 6, 1981 which stated, *inter alia:*

> The State Department said today that it had confirmed reports that the leader of an independent army in Lebanon was threatening to shell the town of Sidon unless the Lebanese Government paid him $5 million in ransom.
> A State Department spokesman, William J. Dyess, said the United States was "deeply concerned and appalled" by what he called a "criminal" act by Maj. Saad Haddad, a former officer of the Lebanese Army.[299]

The prohibition upon terrorism, also firmly established in customary law, has been codified in article 33 of the Civilians Convention. It provides concerning protected civilian persons: "Collective penalities and likewise all measures of intimidation or of terrorism are prohibited." There are many types of terrorism which have been directed at the civilians in Lebanon who are protected by the Convention. Article 33 also adds a prohibition upon reprisals "against protected persons and their property." Consequently, any kind of terrorism which is directed at civilians may not be justified on the ground that it is a claimed reprisal to a prior unlawful act of the opposing party to the conflict.

The immunity of noncombatants from direct attack is one of the most fundamental rules of the international law of armed conflict. It is almost universally accepted as binding customary law. Professor Lauterpacht has set forth the principle this way:

---

293. See, *e.g.,* E. Cody, "Israelis Encourage Irregular Forces," Wash. Post, July 2, 1982, p. A24, cols. 1-3.
294. New York Times, Aug. 18, 1982, p. 6, cols. 1-6.
295. *Id.* at cols. 1-2.
296. *Id.* at col. 3.
297. *Id.* at col. 1.
298. *Id.* at col. 5.
299. New York Times, March 6, 1981, p. A5, cols. 4-6.

Nevertheless it is in that prohibition, which is a clear rule of law, of intentional terrorization—or destruction—of a civilian population as an avowed or obvious object of attack that lies the last vestige of the claim that war can be legally regulated at all. Without that irreducible principle of restraint there is no limit to the licence and depravity of force.[300]

This basic rule is reflected in the United States Air Force official publication, *International Law—The Conduct of Armed Conflict and Air Operations.*[301] It states under the heading, "General Restrictions on Aerial Bombardment: Principle of Immunity of Civilians":

> The civilian population and individual civilians enjoy general protection against dangers arising from military operations. To give effect to this protection, the following specific rules must be observed.
> (a) The civilian population as such, as well as individual civilians, shall not be made the object of attack. Acts or threats of violence which have the primary object of spreading terror among the civilian population are prohibited.
> (b) Civilian objects shall not be made the object of attack. Civilian objects are all objects which are not military objectives. In case of doubt whether an object which is normally dedicated to civilian purposes, such as a house or other dwelling or a school, is being used to make an effective contribution to military action, it shall be presumed not to be so used.[302]

One of the most characteristic features of the Israeli attack-invasion of June-August 1982 was the use of the massive fire power of its armed forces in target area attacks and in attacks specifically directed at civilian targets such as the refugee camps and hospitals.[303] The reports concerning attacks upon civilians and civilian objects are numerous and only a few examples will be considered in the ensuing analysis.

All accounts agree that there were a large number of civilians killed and wounded in the Israeli military attack upon Sidon on the coast of Lebanon, south of Beirut.[304] Mr. Eric Pace reported in the New York Times on June 17, 1982 in an article headed "In Sidon, 80 More Bodies for a Vast Bulldozed Pit."[305] The 80 additional bodies were stated to be Lebanese citizens.[306] The article continued:

> In a patch of open land in the battle-scarred center of Sidon, 200 yards from the Israeli military government headquarters, a dusty bulldozer was spreading dirt over the bodies of civilians in a pit 60 yards long, 10 to 15 yards wide and up to 15 feet deep.[307]

* * *

---

300. "The Problem of the Revision of the Law of War," 29 *Brit. Y.B. Int'l L.* 360, 369 (1952).
301. U.S.A.F. Pamphlet 110-31 (1976).
302. *Id.* at para. 5-3.
303. *E.g.,* Int'l Herald Tribune, Aug. 13, 1982, p. 1, cols. 1-6.
304. Even the lowest estimation, that of Israel, is substantial. The Israeli Foreign Ministry announced on June 22 that there were 400 civilians killed and 1,500 wounded in Sidon alone. New York Times, June 23, 1982, p. A8, cols. 2-4 at col. 3.
305. New York Times, June 17, 1982, p. A21, cols. 1-5.
306. *Id.* at col. 1.
307. *Id.* at cols. 2-3.

At the military headquarters, housed in a labor union building, the Israeli civil affairs administrator for Sidon, Maj. Arnon Mozer, estimated that the Lebanese civilian death toll in Sidon was 400 at most. He indicated that the plan was to bury them in the pit.[308]

Mr. Jonathan Randal reported from Sidon in the Washington Post on June 19, 1982 under the headline, "Sidon's Dead are Still Uncounted."[309] The article stated:

> No one has yet bothered to identify the dead in the basement of the secondary school in Qanaya neighborhood. Still entombed in their makeshift shelter that failed when Israeli bombs fell here last week, they have been dusted with white disinfectant and are swarming with flies.
>
> Nor has anyone counted the corpses in this or other smaller mass graves around the city. Lying in the 50-by-30 foot space beneath the school there are anywhere from 100, according to neighbors, to 260, according to Sidon doctors.
>
> Most of the dead apparently were women and children who had fled their homes at Tyre, 22 miles to the south along the coast, when the Israelis invaded Lebanon June 8.[310]

During and after the invasion of southern Lebanon, various press reports indicated the inadequacy of Israeli claimed attempts to minimize the widespread destruction of civilian human and material values. For example, Ms. Trudy Rubin reported in the Christian Science Monitor on July 15, 1982 under the headline "Largest Palestinian Camp Now a 'Wasteland of Rubble' " concerning the Ain Hilweh (Sweet Spring) camp which was the largest Palestinian refugee camp in Lebanon with at least 25,000 residents.[311] The article stated that Israeli military officials insisted that they warned civilians by loudspeaker and air dropped pamphlets to leave before the final attack on the camp and that they delayed the attack in an attempt to negotiate its surrender.[312] The Israeli claim that they "had no alternative" but to bomb and shell the camp prior to the entry of tanks and other military vehicles was disputed by surviving residents of the camp who stated that the bombing continued while the leaflets were being dropped.[313] Israeli military sources said that the methods of attack employed resulted in "few casualties" to themselves.[314]

The Jerusalem Post International Edition of August 15, 1982 carried an article concerning the Rashidiye camp based on the findings of an Israeli academician, Dr. Zvi Lanir of the Tel Aviv University Center for Strategic Studies.[315] The article reported that the Israeli armed forces had not only destroyed the military infrastructure of the PLO "but also a very extensive socio-economic system which had supported the bulk of the Palestinian population there."[316] Dr. Lanir pointed out that an effective concrete shelter was beyond the means of most residents of the Rashidiye Camp but that it was "increasingly necessary as IDF [Israel Defense Forces] attacks on PLO bases in and around Rashidiye

---

308. *Id.* at cols. 3-4.
309. Wash. Post, June 19, 1982, p. A1, col. 2, cont. p. A21, cols. 1-6.
310. *Id.* at p. A1, col. 2.
311. Christian Sci. Monitor, July 15, 1982, p. 13, cols. 1-3.
312. *Id.* at col. 1.
313. *Id.* at col. 2.
314. *Id.*
315. Jerusalem Post, Int'l Ed., Aug. 15-21, 1982, p. 12, cols. 1-5, cont. p. 13, cols. 1-5.
316. *Id.* at p. 12, col. 1.

became more common."[317] The article stated that the PLO undertook to build shelters for the residents of the camp,[318] and it continued:

> A visit to Rashidiye reveals that one in every three houses has, in fact, been destroyed, ostensibly because it contained what the IDF escort describes as a "bunker." Lanir draws attention to the curious unwillingness of the IDF to recognize that there was an authentic need for shelters in the camp, and even though some of them may indeed have contained weapons or even explosives, the primary purpose of most of them was clearly to protect civilians when the camp came under bombardment.
>
> The provision of the best medical care available and the construction of shelters were clearly high-priority projects for the PLO in the camps.[319]

Dr. Lanir was also reported to state that the approximately 9,000 men being held at the Ansar prison camp as "terrorists" have as many as 60,000 civilian relatives in the area and that these people "are becoming increasingly hostile to Israel, as they fail to understand why their menfolk are still being held."[320] The article continued by pointing out the hazardous situation of Palestinian civilians:

> The danger of a massacre of the Palestinian population in South Lebanon should not be dismissed, Lanir warns—and if it ever occurs, those who survived would provide the breeding ground for a Palestinian liberation movement that, born of desperation, might be even worse than the PLO.[321]

A sense of realism concerning the early bombing of Beirut can be achieved from reading a dispatch by Jonathan C. Randal of June 10 which was published in the Washington Post the next day.[322] He described June 10 as "the most intensive air bombardment to date against Beirut."[323] His report referred to attacks on civilian objects and persons:

> In one sequence of bombing runs, observed from the hills above the airport, the warplanes hit a Datsun car depot, the Pepsi-Cola bottling plant, a farm equipment warehouse and a tin can factory just to the east of the runways where four jetliners were parked.
>
> Later, the Israeli aircraft bombed refugee camps at Bourj el Brajneh and Chatila Sabra, the guerrilla office near the Arab University and a previously spared neighborhood less than 200 yards from the dividing line between the Moslem and Christian sections of the city.[324]

During the negotiations leading to the evacuation of the Palestinian armed forces from Beirut, Mr. Robert Fisk reported from the scene in The Times (London) on August 13, 1982 under the headline: "Beirut shudders under 10-hour aerial attack." The article stated, *inter alia:*

> In 10 hours of non-stop air raids, the Israelis poured high explosive bombs on to the two Palestinian camps in west Beirut yesterday in an apparent attempt to destroy them before Palestinian guerrillas begin to evacuate the city.[325]

* * *

---

317. *Id.* at col. 5.
318. *Id.*
319. *Id.*
320. *Id.* at p. 13, cols. 4-5.
321. *Id.* at col. 5.
322. "Waves of Israeli Jets Bomb Lebanon's Besieged Capital," Wash. Post, June 11, 1982, p. A1, cols. 5-6, cont. p. A19, cols. 1-5.
323. *Id.* at p. A1, col. 1.
324. *Id.* at col. 2.
325. The Times (London), Aug. 13, 1982, p. 4, cols. 1-3, at col. 1.

> If the Israeli air attacks were predictable, their ferocity was unexpected. For much of the day...fighter-bomber aircraft flew only 100 ft. over the rooftops, unloading hundreds of tons of high explosives.[326]

Article 31 of the Civilians Convention broadly prohibits "physical or moral coercion" against protected persons and, in particular, any such coercion which is designed "to obtain information from them or from third parties." Article 17 of the P.O.W. Convention contains a similiar protection against physical or moral coercion for the purpose of obtaining information. According to numerous on the scene press reports, one of the principal purposes of Israeli conducted interrogations of prisoners was to obtain information concerning the identities of the "Palestinian sympathizers" who were hunted throughout southern Lebanon and in west Beirut.[327]

Like several other provisions of the Civilians Convention, article 32 is a reaction to the practices particularly associated with the Nazis and reflects a determination to avoid their repetition. It provides in full:

> The High Contracting Parties specifically agree that each of them is prohibited from taking any measure of such a character as to cause the physical suffering or extermination of protected persons in their hands. This prohibition applies not only to murder, torture, corporal punishment, mutilation and medical or scientific experiments not necessitated by the medical treatment of a protected person, but also to any other measures of brutality whether applied by civilian or military agents.

According to its terms, this is a unilateral obligation undertaken by each of the state parties to the Convention including the State of Israel. In spite of the narrow wording of the provision as based upon the agreement of "the High Contracting Parties," the basic prohibition upon "murder, torture," and "any other measures of brutality" must be interpreted as also being applicable to all factual parties to the conflict in order to effectuate the humanitarian purpose of the Convention. The actions of the Government of Israel and its agents which have been amply documented include, *inter alia,* acts of murder, torture, and corporal punishment.[328]

The prohibition on pillage (or looting) is firmly established in customary law and it is codified in article 33(2) of the Civilians Convention: "Pillage is prohibited." The Washington Post on September 29, 1982 carried an article by Mr. Loren Jenkins which gave the details of a long list of thefts, as well as destruction of the property which was not taken, and the spreading of feces in both residences and business establishments by the Israeli Army.[329] Many residents of Beirut complained of the theft or irreparable damage to items such as artifacts which were irreplaceable.[330] Mr. Salim Salam, the managing director of Middle East Airlines, reported massive thefts of its properties during the time that the Israeli Army was in control of Beirut International Airport. The items, *inter alia,* included the entire computer reservations system, six minibuses, four Land

---

326. *Id.*
> Israeli forces attacking West Beirut have battered the city's small Jewish community, shelled its only synagogue and sent dozens of Jewish families fleeing for safety....

Wash. Post, Aug. 12, 1982, p. A25, cols. 4-5 at col. 5.
327. The text accompanying *supra* notes 288 and 289.
328. *E.g.,* the text accompanying *supra* notes 252-259.
329. Wash. Post, Sept. 29, 1982, p. A15, cols. 1-2.
330. *Id.* at col. 2.

Rovers, as well as numerous smaller items including aircraft mechanics' tools.[331] Mr. Jenkins corroborated the facts concerning the spreading of feces in a Beirut mosque.[332] In another article, the Beirut reporter of Agence France Presse, Mr. Xavier Baron, wrote that several apartments including his own in the Hamra district of west Beirut had been ransacked "and the only people who had access were Israeli troops."[333]

The properties of the Palestine Liberation Organization were given particular attention. The offices of the PLO were ransacked, with valuables and records stolen.[334] The PLO Research Center, a publisher of academic works in English and Arabic, was stripped of everything in it including irreplaceable manuscripts and its 25,000 volume library.[335] Dr. Sabri Jiryis, the Director of the Center, estimated material losses at $1.5 million.[336]

Reference has previously been made to truckloads of blindfolded and handcuffed Palestinian and Lebanese men being transported to unknown destinations in the State of Israel.[337] Among the men so transported there were probably substantial numbers of Palestinian and Lebanese civilians. If even one civilian was included, it would be a violation of article 49(1) of the Civilians Convention which provides that:

> Individual or mass forcible transfers, as well as deportations of protected persons from occupied territory to the territory of the Occupying Power, or to that of any other country occupied or not, are prohibited, regardless of their motive.

The second paragraph of the same article provides that the occupying power may undertake the partial or total evacuation of the population of a particular area if the security of the population or imperative military reasons require that it be done. Even then, such transfers may not take protected civilians outside the occupied territory unless it is impossible to care for them adequately in the occupied territory. It is also provided that: "Persons thus evacuated shall be transferred back to their homes as soon as hostilities in the area in question have ceased."[338] It is clear that the Israeli deportation of civilians into Israel is not permitted by any of the exceptions which are set forth in the article.

Following the destruction of the Ain Hilweh camp in southern Lebanon, Yaacov Gravinsky, an assistant to Israeli Cabinet Minister Jaacov Meridor, who was supervising the Israeli relief aid for Lebanon, said that the refugees were being denied tents for temporary shelter "because this would turn into a 'permanent' solution."[339] The United Nations Relief and Works Agency (UNRWA), which is responsible for the refugees, says about 35,000 persons in Sidon and

---

331. *Id.* at col. 1.
332. *Id.*
333. *Id.* at col. 2.
334. New York Times, Oct. 1, 1982, p. A8, cols. 5-6.
335. *Id.* at col. 5.
336. *Id.* The cumulative destruction was a violation of the Hague Convention for the Protection of Cultural Property in the Event of Armed Conflict of 14 May 1954 to which Israel became a party on October 3, 1957. The Convention appears in Schindler & Toman, *supra* note 171, at 661.
337. The text accompanying *supra* notes 250-251.
338. Art. 49(2).
339. *Supra* note 311 at p. 13, col. 3.

Tyre area are homeless.[340] The subsequent Israeli decision to permit the tents was stated to have come after weeks of negotiations with UNRWA.[341] According to the report of Mr. Edward Walsh in the Washington Post on August 27, 1982, Cabinet Minister Meridor stressed that this was merely a "temporary solution" and "Israel remains determined to see the camps dismantled and the refugees dispersed....[342]

There have been a number of claims concerning casualty figures for the attack-invasion. An article in the New York Times on June 23, 1982 referred to inconsistent casualty figures concerning particular areas:

> Israel's Foreign Ministry announced today that a total of 460 to 470 civilians had been killed and 1,600 wounded in fighting in southern Lebanon, excluding Beirut, for which the Israelis have no casualty figures.[343]
>
> The head of the Red Cross delegation in Beirut, Francesco Noseda, said June 12 that his organization had estimated the number of people killed in Sidon alone had reached as high as 1,500. He said the estimates of the number of homeless in southern Lebanon were as high as 600,000.[344]

There were also inconsistent casualty figures for the entire attack-invasion. The Washington Post on September 3, 1982 quoted the independent Beirut newspaper An Nahar as listing a total of 48,000 with 17,825 killed and 30,203 wounded.[345] A total figure of 2,000 casualties with most stated to be military was attributed to Israeli Defense Minister Sharon.[346] An unidentified relief official was quoted as stating that studies by his organization indicated "that about 80 percent of the injured were civilian and only 20 percent military."[347] Whatever the figure of civilian casualties is ultimately determined to be, those casualties which are due to direct attack upon concentrations of civilians, civilian objects, hospitals and medical personnel, have been the result of violations of the applicable provisions of international law. The reports of the contemporary factual events upon which this analysis is based are fully supported by the findings of the International Commission chaired by Sean MacBride.[348]

D. International Law Limitations Upon Weapons

1. The Legal Criteria Concerning Weapons

The prohibitory rules concerning weapons should be considered in the broader context of the basic principles limiting the conduct of hostilities. These principles are military necessity and humanity. Military necessity permits a party to the conflict to apply that degree and kind of regulated force not otherwise prohibited by the law, required for the partial or complete submission of an enemy.[349] The closely related principle of humanity prohibits the employment of

---

340. *Id.*
341. Wash. Post, Aug. 27, 1982, p. A1, cols. 2-3 at col. 2.
342. *Id.* at cols. 2-3.
343. *Supra* note 304 at p. A8, col. 1.
344. *Id.* at col. 2.
345. Wash. Post, Sept. 3, 1982, p. A22, cols. 1-3 at col. 1.
346. *Id.* at col. 2.
347. *Id.* at col. 3.
348. *MacBride Comm., supra* note 252 at 51-65, 68-76.
349. U.S. Air Force Pamphlet 110-31, *International Law—The Conduct of Armed Conflict and Air Operations,* para. 1-3(a)(1) (1976).

any kind or degree of force which is not necessary to achieve a lawful military objective.[350] Both basic principles protect important value interests of the world community. Until war and hostilities are abolished, the basic principles reflect the interest of states in conducting war or hostilities (at least for defensive purposes), but in conducting them with the least possible destruction of human and material values. It is wanton and unreasonable destruction which is made illegal by the principles of military necessity and humanity. The application of either principle as if the other did not exist would result in unbalanced decision. It is essential to apply each principle in the light of the other if the common interests of states are to be honored. From this perspective, each principle may be usefully conceived as an element of a larger composite principle which may be formulated as the minimization of the unnecessary destruction of human and material values.[351]

A determination of what is excessive destruction must be made by reference to the doctrine of proportionality as it is applied to combat situations. Proportionality, in this sense, postulates that there must be a reasonable relationship between the lawful destructiveness of the weapon and its ancillary or collateral effects as set forth in the principles of military necessity and humanity.[352] Its prohibited ancillary effects include both excessive killing and wounding of enemy combatants and of civilians as an incident to the lawful attacks on the military targets. The concept of proportionality is difficult to apply to borderline situations because the comparisons involved are between decidedly different values. The specific context attempts to assess the relative weights to be given to innocent human lives as opposed to military efficiency in achieving a particular military objective. The practical, but unfortunate, result of this is that in most borderline situations some destruction of civilian values is usually accepted as lawful. However, the utility of the proportionality doctrine is demonstrated by its application in relatively extreme situations such as where the ancillary destruction of civilian values is so great as to be obviously disproportionate to the military objective sought. It is in this type of context that the doctrine is useful in prohibiting such unreasonble or unnecessary destruction of human and material values.

A basic distinction exists between the juridical status of a weapon itself and the uses to which the weapon is put.[353] Customary law or treaties make some weapons illegal *per se,* and this has the result of prohibiting their use under any circumstances. In addition, any weapon may be used in an unlawful manner such as by directing it at civilians rather than at lawful military objectives. It is important to be aware that the doctrine of proportionality has no relevance to situations where civilians are made direct objects of attack. The unequivocal rule prohibiting direct attacks upon civilians in any circumstances is applicable.

The principal treaty law on the subject of weapons is in the Hague Regulations of 1907[354] which are now binding customary law. Many of the 1907 Regulations simply repeat the 1899 Hague Regulations with occasional minor changes in

---

350. *Id.* at para. 1-3(a)(2). The legal principle of humanity is supported by the military principle of economy of force. W.T. Mallison, *Studies in the Law of Naval Warfare* 20 (U.S. Naval War College, 1966).
351. McDougal & Feliciano, *Law and Minimum World Public Order* 530 (1961).
352. *Id.* at 241-44.
353. W.T. Mallison, *supra* note 350 at 156.
354. 36 U.S. Stat. 2277, Schindler & Toman, *supra* note 171, at 57-92.

words, and some of them were probably customary law when they were written in 1899.[355]

Article 22 of both the 1899 and 1907 Regulations provides: "The right of belligerents to adopt means of injuring the enemy is not unlimited." Article 23 of the 1907 Regulations sets forth more specific prohibitions concerning weapons under this general guideline of article 22. The relevant provisions of article 23 state:

> In addition to the prohibitions provided by special Conventions, it is especially forbidden—
>
> a. To employ poison or poisoned weapons;
> b. To kill or wound treacherously individuals belonging to the hostile nation or army;
>
> * * *
>
> e. To employ arms, projectiles, or material calculated to cause unnecessary suffering. . . .

These provisions are identical with the similarly numbered provisions of the 1899 Regulations except that the last clause of paragraph "e" reads "material of a nature to cause superfluous injury" in the 1899 Regulations. In the situation where a lawful military objective is attacked, articles 22 and 23 together prohibit excessive incidental or collateral injury to military personnel and civilians.

Weapons which have been made illegal *per se* by customary law without regard to the uses to which they may be put include projectiles filled with glass, plastic, or other materials which are undetectable through the use of medical procedures.[356] Such weapons are also in violation of subsections "b" and "e" of article 23 because of their characteristics involving treachery and causing unnecessary suffering. Other examples of weapons which are similarly prohibited are booby traps disguised as harmless objects such as mechanical pencils or pens, watches, and various kinds of trinkets and toys. These weapons embody a treacherous form of attack on both enemy combatants and civilians. In addition, they are designed to cause indiscriminate as well as unnecessary suffering to those who are victimized by them. Booby traps appearing to be trinkets or toys are particularly offensive because children are their most likely victims. The official U.S. Air Force Manual states that "mines in the nature of booby traps are frequently unlawfully used" and includes in this category:

> portable booby traps in the form of fountain pens, watches and trinkets which suggest treachery and unfairly risk injuries to civilians likely to be attracted to the objects.[357]

2. Application of the Criteria Concerning Weapons

The legality of two particular weapons widely used in the attack-invasion of Lebanon must be questioned under the principles set forth in both the customary and the treaty law. These are the cluster bombs and the phosphorous incendiary bombs. While such weapons used against a military target under certain conditions may not be illegal *per se,* the legality of their use in an indiscriminate attack on a heavily populated area must be examined under the relevant criteria.

---

355. 2 *Oppenheim's International Law* 340 (7th ed., Lauterpacht, 1952).
356. See Swedish Working Group Study, *Conventional Weapons: Their Deployment and Effects From Humanitarian Aspect* 165 (Swedish Foreign Affairs Ministry, 1973).
357. *Supra* note 349 at para 6-6(d).

Cluster bombs are a type of unit in which hundreds of smaller bombs are packed into a cannister dropped from aircraft.[358] Mr. Robert Fisk describes an attack by cluster bombs in the Times of London on August 13, 1982:

> By late afternoon, the Israeli jets were dropping bombs never previously seen over such heavily residential districts, projectiles that streaked from the aircraft and exploded at 50 ft. intervals in the sky in clouds of smoke, apparently spraying smaller bombs in a wider arc around. Most of these weapons were dropped in the district of Corniche Mazraa, the boulevard that runs from the museum—where Israeli tanks are positioned—through the heart of West Beirut.[359]

A report in the Christian Science Monitor, on July 20, 1982, stated that:

> The effective coverage area for a single CBU is reported by James Dunnican in "How to Make War: A Comprehensive Guide to Modern Warfare" to be 50 meters wide by 200 meters long. Therefore they are difficult to deliver with pinpoint accuracy in areas where military targets are close to civilian populations.[360]

An article in the Philadephia Inquirer entitled "Israel criticized for use of indiscriminate bombs" reports several examples of the effects of these bombs on children and other civilians.[361] Dr. Ammal Shamma, Chief of Pediatrics at Barbir Hospital in Beirut, is an American of Lebanese birth trained at Johns Hopkins University. She acted as Head of Emergency Services during the attack on Beirut. She is quoted as saying in reference to the victims of cluster bombs:

> "So many amputations. I have never seen it so bad. The number of people who lose limbs, the number of bodies that come in in pieces. We've had children literally brought in in pieces. It's the most hideous group of injuries I've ever seen in my career."[362]

Concern over possible misuse of U.S. supplied cluster bombs against civilians in the 1978 Israeli invasion into Lebanon is reported to have resulted in a special agreement whereby Israel pledged not to use the weapons except in full-scale wars in defense of Israeli territory and against organized armies.[363] Another source stated that the weapons would only be used "against fortified military positions."[364] An article in the New York Times of June 30, 1982 reports that while the agreement itself is secret, "United States officials said today that Israel had agreed in 1978 not to use American-made cluster bomb units except in combat with 'two or more Arab states'...".[365] The special provisions governing the supply of these weapons are an indication of United States awareness of the unique destructiveness and potentially devastating effect they can have when used in an area inhabited by civilians. A Pentagon spokesman is quoted as saying that, "the United States is opposed to the use of any weapons that 'kill indiscriminately,' which would characterize them as 'terror weapons'."[366] Concurrent with numerous reports by foreign correspondents on the scene that Israel had used

358. See "Cluster Bombs: How They Work," *MacBride Comm.* 230-37 containing description and diagrams. See also "How a Cluster Bomb Works," New York Times, June 20, 1982, p. A12, cols. 1-4.
359. The Times (London), Aug. 13, 1982, p. 4, col. 2.
360. Christian Sci. Monitor, July 20, 1982, p. 1, col. 1, cont. p. 8, cols. 1-3 at col. 3. "CBU" refers to cluster bomb units.
361. Philadelphia Inquirer, June 30, 1982, p. 1-A, cols. 1-3, cont. p. 10-A, cols. 1-4.
362. *Id.* at p. 10-A, col. 1.
363. Christian Sci. Monitor, July 20, 1982, p. 1, col. 1, cont. p. 8, cols. 1-2, at col. 1.
364. Wash. Post, June 28, 1982, p. A15, col. 5.
365. New York Times, *supra* note 358 at A-12, col. 1.
366. *Supra* note 361, p. 10-A, col. 4.

cluster bombs against heavily populated areas in the 1982 attack-invasion, Israeli Major General Aharon Yariv denied such use: "They were not used against civilians. I mean areas where there were concentrations of civilians."[367] An article in the Christian Science Monitor of October 8, 1982 stated that:

> Mr. Shai of the Israeli Embassy [Washington, D.C.] says that Israel used CBUs in Lebanon as "an antipersonnel weapon."
>
> "It doesn't do anything to buildings or tanks," he says. "But it does do a lot to people."[368]

As a result of the evidence of the Israeli use of this weapon in areas of Lebanon with heavy concentrations of civilians, President Reagan suspended shipment of such ammunition to Israel following a secret review stated to concern violations of the agreements under which the weapons were supplied. Mr. John Goshko reported in the Washington Post of July 28, 1982:

> Although Israel has denied it broke agreements restricting use of the U.S.—supplied cluster units, the still-secret review is understood to have concluded that some violations did occur.[369]

It is clear that a number of basic principles of international law have been violated by the use of this weapon in the attacks on populated areas. The weapon is indiscriminate, it causes injuries which are excessive in relation to any possible military objective that might be accomplished by its use, and it was directed at areas where the main impact was on civilians.

A similar conclusion has been reached by the International Commission chaired by Sean MacBride:

> The Commission concludes on the evidence before it that there was extensive use of fragmentation weapons [the term used by the Commission to refer to cluster bombs] in areas where there was and is a high concentration of civilians; that in light of the widespread impact and destructive effects of these weapons, and in some cases, their delayed-action nature, indiscriminate death and injury to combatants and civilians occurred. The Commission concludes that this use of fragmentation weapons by the IDF was contrary to the principle of discrimination and was thus a violation of the laws of war.[370]

The other weapon which should be specifically examined is the phosphorous incendiary bomb which again, while probably not illegal against specific military targets, violates international law when used against a heavily populated area. The Times of London, in an article entitled "Robert Fisk reports on Israel's use of phosphorous bombs in Beirut," described this weapon:

> Phosphorous shells and bombs are regarded as routine ammunition in most western armies, which use the projectiles as artillery markers or smokescreens. However, their use is generally confined to open battlefields, and three protocols agreed at a 1980 United Nations convention in Geneva contain broad restrictions on the use of incendiary weapons against military objectives located in residential areas of towns and cities.[371]

---

367. Wash. Post, June 28, 1982, p. A15, col. 5.
368. Christian Sci. Monitor, Oct. 8, 1982, p. 5, col. 2.
369. "Reagan Bans Indefinitely Cluster Shells for Israel," Wash. Post, July 28, 1982, p. A16, cols. 5-6, at col. 5.
370. *MacBride Comm., supra* note 252 at 97.
371. The Times (London), Aug. 2, 1982, p. 8, cols. 2-5 at cols. 3-4.

The reference here is to the three weapons protocols of 1980. These protocols were negotiated with the participation of military experts and representatives of all the major military powers.[372] Protocol III requires that civilians not be attacked by incendiary weapons.[373] It is a modern codification reflecting the customary law prohibiting attacks on civilians as well as the treaty law of the Hague Regulations of 1907 forbidding the use of weapons which cause unnecessary suffering.

An article in the Christian Science Monitor on August 19, 1982 reported:

> In west Beirut, phosphorous shells and bombs have crashed into the main street, Hamra, hitting banks, local newspapers, and foreign news offices. They have plowed into two hospitals, a Red Cross building, and hundreds of apartments.[374]
>
> * * *
>
> Those used in the city have crashed into areas where Palestinian civilians had taken refuge, such as Hamra.[375]
>
> * * *
>
> They say that without the proper [medical] supplies, the only way to stop the burning is either to cut the burning tissue away or amputate. No one here has supplies.[376]
>
> * * *
>
> Relief workers are reporting an unusually high incidence of amputations in west Beirut—particularly they say, among civilians.[377]
>
> * * *
>
> "Usually war is on the battlefield," Dr. Russli [a Canadian Born Norwegian physician with experience in Cambodia] said. "Seventy percent of my patients are civilians."[378]

There are numerous other press reports of the injuries created by the phosphorous burns which cannot be extinguished and continue to burn the victim. For example, an article by Loren Jenkins in the Washington Post of August 20, 1982 under the headline "Beirut Phosphorus Victim: 'I Felt I Was Suddenly on Fire' " reported:

> The wounds are distinctive and much harder to treat than ordinary burns, the doctors say, in part because phosphorus sticks to the skin and can burn for hours. It cannot be extinguished by water, which causes a chemical reaction that makes the wound burn more. Like the Aytawi family [described in detail in an earlier part of the article], victims often arrive at the hospital with smoke still pouring out of their bodies from internal burns as well as skin injuries.[379]

Even if this weapon is not illegal *per se*, since its accepted use is as a flare or marker in an open area, its use as an anti-personnel weapon in a heavily

---

372. The State of Israel and the United States were represented.
373. "Protocol III on Prohibitions or Restrictions on the Use of Incendiary Weapons" in Final Report of the U.N. Conference on the Use of Certain Conventional Weapons Which May be Deemed to be Excessively Injurious or to Have Indiscriminate Effects, A/CONF. 95/15 at pp. 16-17 (27 Oct. 1980). None of the three Protocols has been ratified thus far by Israel or the United States, but both states are bound by the customary law reflected in them.
374. Christian Sci. Monitor, Aug. 19, 1982, p. 3, cols. 1-4 at col. 2.
375. *Id.*
376. *Id.* at col. 3.
377. *Id.*
378. *Id.* at col. 4.
379. Wash. Post, Aug. 20, 1982, p. A1, cols. 3-4 at col. 4.

populated area with the resulting extreme injuries to civilians must be characterized as illegal.

The International Commission, after examining the Israeli use of these weapons stated:

> The Commission concludes on the evidence before it that the IDF did shell Beirut extensively using phosphorus shells in areas where there was a high concentration of civilians; that the incendiary effects of these shells on civilian objects and particularly on the civilian population was considerable. The Commission therefore finds that the use of these incendiary weapons by the IDF was contrary to the principle of discrimination and is a violation of the laws of war.[380]

The United States Air Force Manual states:

> International law does not require that a weapon's effects be strictly confined to the military objectives against which it is directed, but it does restrict weapons whose foreseeable effects result in unlawful disproportionate injury to civilians or damage to civilian objects.[381]
>
> * * *
>
> In particular, the potential capacity of fire to spread must be considered in relation to the rules protecting civilians and civilian objects....For example, incendiary weapons should be avoided in urban areas to the extent that other weapons are available and effective. Additionally, incendiary weapons must not be used so as to cause unnecessary suffering.[382]

This analysis based upon the customary and treaty law makes it clear that the use of two of the weapons (cluster bombs and phosphorus shells) employed by the Israeli military in Lebanon, including the attack on the city of Beirut, was contrary to international law.

The International Commission has reached the same conclusion. Its report states:

> The Commission is of the view that, on the evidence, the horrific extent and nature of these wounds and death inflicted by these weapons was unnecessary; and that there are limits which humanity places on the use of weapons causing human suffering of the types described. The Commission concludes that the use by the IDF of fragmentation weapons [cluster bombs] and phosphorus shells in the urban centres of civilian population of Lebanon violated the international legal principle of humanity in the conduct of war.[383]

There are also reports of children's toys and other attractive objects containing explosives which injure or maim.[384] In addition to violating the prohibition against treacherous weapons, these objects appear to be part of an attempt to terrorize the population, contrary to the prohibition of the use of terror against the civilian population in the Geneva Civilians Convention,[385] and to place extra

---

380. *MacBride Comm.* 99.
381. *Supra* note 349 at para. 6-3(c).
382. *Id.* at para. 6-6(c).
383. *MacBride Comm.* 103.
384. Pat McDonnell, "Young Victims of a Savage War," *The Middle East,* No. 95, pp. 28-29 (Sept. 1982). The Christian Sci. Monitor, Nov. 2, 1982, p. 1, col. 4, cont. p. 7, cols. 2-3 cites military experts as saying that unexploded cluster bomblets are a particular hazard to children because they appear to be toys. The article reports a number of specific cases of such injuries and deaths to children.
385. *Supra* note 182, art. 33(1).

stress on medical facilities which were seriously damaged and handicapped from the beginning of the attack-invasion. These conditions are described, *inter alia*, in an article entitled "Young Victims of a Savage War" by Pat McDonnell, appearing in *The Middle East* magazine:

> The exhausted hospital director, Dr. Ibrahim Alway, said the hospital had 400 patients, 80 per cent of whom where civilians. His staff had treated victims of booby-trapped toys, napalm, phosphorous and cluster bombs.[386]

It is clear that booby-trapped toys and trinkets are illegal *per se*.

E. The Crime of Genocide

1. The Elements of the Crime

The question of whether or not the Israeli attacks on the Palestinians during the summer and fall of 1982, including Israeli implication in the Beirut massacre, constitutes an act of genocide has been raised and must be addressed. The matter was raised specifically in the United Nations General Assembly where, while accepting the decision not to act on the proposal that the credentials of the State of Israel be rejected, a group of 50 countries submitted a collective written reservation in a letter to the General Assembly on October 26, 1982.[387] Among the matters included in the letter was the "crime of genocide" which it said had been committed against the Palestinians.

The Convention on the Prevention and Punishment of the Crime of Genocide[388] was drafted following the Second World War. During that War, the Nazis, in addition to individual acts of murder, killed groups of people selected on the basis of their national, ethnic, racial or religious identification. The International Military Tribunal acted on the postulate that such killing of groups was in violation of pre-existing law and that the perpetrators incurred individual criminal responsibility.[389] The drafters of the Convention were motivated by a desire to prevent mass killings in the future.

The second, third, and fourth articles of the Convention state the elements of the crime of genocide:

> Art. 2. In the present Convention, genocide means any of the following acts committed with intent to destroy, in whole or in part, a national, ethnical, racial or religious group, as such:

---

386. *The Middle East, supra* note 384.
387. U.N. Press Release WS/1099, Oct. 29, 1982, p. 3.
388. 78 U.N.T.S. 277, Schindler & Toman, *supra* note 171, at 171.
389. The Charter of the International Military Tribunal at Nuremberg defined crimes against humanity as, *inter alia,* "murder, extermination, enslavement, deportation, and other inhumane acts committed against any civilian population, before or during the war." Charter of the International Military Tribunal art. 6(c) in 1 I.M.T. 10 at 11. The Judgment of the Tribunal held that mass murders within the definition had taken place and those defendants who had participated in them directly or indirectly were adjudged to be guilty. *Id.* at 232-38.

(a) Killing members of the group;

(b) Causing serious bodily or mental harm to members of the group;

(c) Deliberately inflicting on the group conditions of life calculated to bring about its physical destruction in whole or in part;

(d) Imposing measures intended to prevent births within the group;

(e) Forcibly transferring children of the group to another group.

Art. 3. The following acts shall be punishable:

(a) Genocide;

(b) Conspiracy to commit genocide;

(c) Direct and public incitement to commit genocide;

(d) Attempt to commit genocide;

(e) Complicity in genocide.

Art. 4. Persons committing genocide or any of the other acts enumerated in Article 3 shall be punished, whether they are constitutionally responsible rulers, public officials or private individuals.

The Convention was approved by General Assembly resolution 260A(III) of December 9, 1948[390] and entered into force on January 12, 1951. Both Lebanon and Israel are parties to it. In its Advisory Opinion of May 28, 1951[391] the International Court of Justice stated that the Genocide Convention was "adopted for a purely humanitarian and civilizing purpose" and that:

> In such a convention the contracting States do not have any interests of their own; they merely have, one and all, a common interest, namely the accomplishment of those high purposes which are the *raison d' être* of the Convention.[392]

There are two elements involved in the definition of the crime of genocide. The first is the commission of certain acts, and the second is the requisite state of mind defined as the "intent to destroy, in whole or in part," a particular identifiable group. The ancillary killings of disproportionate numbers of Palestinian and Lebanese civilians as part of combat operations is contrary to the international law regarding the protection of civilians[393] and may come within the meaning of article 2(a) of the Genocide Convention which refers to the killing of members of a national, ethnical, racial or religious group as such. The reported brutal treatment of detained persons[394] constitutes the "serious bodily or mental harm" referred to in paragraph (b), and the calculated destruction of homes and facilities necessary for the survival of the civilian population[395] may be characterized as deliberately creating the group conditions for the physical destruction referred to in paragraph (c). In addition, one of the results of imprisoning substantially the entire Palestinian adult male population in Lebanon could be interpreted to be to "prevent births within the group" which is referred to in paragraph (d). While each of these actions involves violations of the humanitarian law concerning protected civilian persons and prisoners of war, they may also be referred to as acts of genocide if the requisite intent to destroy a particular group in whole or in part is shown.

---

390. *3 U.N. GAOR, Part I, Annex,* p. 494, Doc. A/760.

391. *Reservations to the Convention on Genocide,* [1951] I.C.J. Reps. 15.

392. *Id.* at 23.

393. Chapter III C *supra.*

394. See the text accompanying notes 252-258.

395. See Chapter III Sections C2 and 3 *supra.*

2. The Application of the Law

On September 15, 1982 Israel moved its troops into West Beirut in violation of its undertaking not to do so.[396] It was claimed that the purpose of this action was to maintain public order and security following the assassination of Lebanese President-elect Bashir Gemayal in East Beirut which was under Israeli military occupation. According to Israeli Defense Minister Sharon, this claim was "only a 'smoke screen' to hide Israel's real intention—the destruction of the remaining Palestinian guerrillas thought still to be in the city."[397]

The grim events of Thursday, Friday, and Saturday, September 16, 17, and 18, 1982 in which at least several hundred[398] helpless civilian women, children and elderly people were slaughtered in the Sabra and Shatila refugee camps brought the issue of genocide sharply into focus. The facts indicate that these people were murdered because they were Palestinians.[339] Mr Ze'ev Schiff, the military correspondent of the independent Israeli newspaper, Ha'aretz, wrote:

> A war crime has been committed in the refugee camps of Beirut. The Falangists executed hundreds or more women, children and old people. What happened was exactly what used to happen in the pogroms against the Jews. It is not true that these atrocities came to our attention only on Saturday afternoon, after foreign correspondents had filed reports on them from Beirut, as is claimed by Israeli spokesmen.[400]

Mr. Schiff points out that his own personal experience in Beirut on those days shows clearly that there was Israeli knowledge of and implication in the events.[401]

The International Committee of the Red Cross (I.C.R.C.) issued a press release on the massacre on September 18, 1982. It stated in part:

ICRC DELEGATES IN BEIRUT HAVE REPORTED THAT HUNDREDS OF CHILDREN, ADOLESCENTS, WOMEN AND OLD PEOPLE HAVE BEEN KILLED IN THE SHATILA QUARTER OF BEIRUT, THEIR CORPSES LYING SCATTERED IN THE STREETS.

---

396. Agreement between Lebanon, the United States, France, Italy, and the PLO entitled "Plan for the Departure from Lebanon of the PLO Leadership, Offices, and Combatants in Beirut," Aug. 19, 1982, U.S. Dept. of State, Bureau of Public Affairs, Current Policy No. 415 (Aug. 1982). Art. 2 provides in full: "A cease-fire in place will be scrupulously observed by all in Lebanon." On Sept. 18, 1982, after learning of the massacre in the refugee camps, President Reagan issued a statement which said, *inter alia,* "[W]e were assured that Israeli forces would not enter West Beirut," Wash. Post, Sept. 19, 1982, p. A16, col. 3.
397. Edward Walsh, "Israeli Army Under Seige: Questions Surrounding Massacre Strain Credibility," Wash. Post, Sept. 26, 1982, p. A21, cols. 1-3 at col. 2. There has been no evidence of the presence of Palestinian combatants in the Beirut refugee camps.
398. The Lebanese Government placed the number killed at "nearly 2000." Christian Sci. Monitor, Oct. 14, 1982, p. 2, cols. 2-3, at col. 3.
399. The hatred of the Phalangists and other ultra-rightist militias toward Palestinians is described in "Phalangist Ties to Massacre Detailed" by Loren Jenkins, Wash. Post, Sept. 30, 1982, p. 1, cols. 2-4, cont. p. A38, cols. 1-6. See also Loren Jenkins, "Unprotected Palestinians Live in Fear," Wash. Post, Sept. 22, 1982, p. A1, cols. 1-2, cont. p. A18, cols. 1-4.
400. "War Crime in Beirut," Ha'aretz, Sept. 20, 1982 translated in *Israeli Mirror* (London), Sept. 22, 1982, pp. 1-2.
401. *Id.* at 2.

THE ICRC HAS ALSO ASCERTAINED THAT WOUNDED PATIENTS HAVE BEEN MURDERED IN THEIR HOSPITAL BEDS, WHILE OTHER PATIENTS AND DOCTORS HAVE BEEN ABDUCTED.

* * *

THE ICRC SOLEMNLY APPEALS TO THE INTERNATIONAL COMMUNITY TO INTERVENE TO PUT AN IMMEDIATE STOP TO THE INTOLERABLE MASSACRE PERPETRATED IN BEIRUT ON WHOLE GROUPS OF PEOPLE AND TO ENSURE THAT THE WOUNDED AND THOSE WHO TREAT THEM BE RESPECTED AND PROTECTED AND THAT THE BASIC RIGHT TO LIVE BE OBSERVED.

FOR YOUR INFORMATION, ICRC HAS REMINDED THE ISRAELI GOVERNMENT THAT, WHOEVER THE AUTHORS OF THESE CRIMES ARE, IT IS THE RESPONSIBILITY OF THE ISRAELI ARMED FORCES ACCORDING TO THE HAGUE AND GENEVA CONVENTIONS, TO TAKE ALL MEASURES TO INSURE PUBLIC ORDER AND SAFETY AND TO PROTECT CIVILIANS AGAINST ACTS OF VIOLENCE IN THE TERRITORIES WHICH THEY CONTROL.[402]

Under the customary law expressed in Hague Convention IV Respecting the Laws and Customs of War on Land,[403] the responsibility of the belligerent occupant for acts taking place within the occupied territory is established. Article 3 of the text of this Convention provides: "It [the belligerent occupant] shall be responsible for all acts committed by persons forming part of its armed forces." Article 29 of the Geneva Civilians Convention[404] provides in comprehensive terms that the party to the conflict responsible for protected persons (in the present situation, it is the belligerent occupant) "is responsible for the treatment accorded to them by its agents."

As stated by the International Commission, it is clear that:

[T]he residents of the camps were 'protected persons' within the meaning of Geneva Convention IV and Israel as an Occupying Power was under a special obligation to prevent the commission of 'outrages' against them.[405]

The question of whether or not the Israeli leadership had the "intent," which is an essential element in the crime of genocide, should be determined judicially. Widely accepted legal definitions of "intent" and related concepts are:

Intent: A mental attitude which can seldom be proved by direct evidence, but must ordinarily be proved by circumstances from which it may be inferred.[406]

Constructive intent: Exists where one should have reasonably expected or anticipated a particular result.[407]

Constructive knowledge: If one by exercise of reasonable care should have known a fact, he is deemed to have had constructive knowledge of such fact.[408]

Using these definitions as criteria, it is necessary to consider the factual circumstances from which Israeli intent may be inferred. It is clear that the Israeli Government made the decision to allow the Phalangists, who were known to have carried out prior attacks involving substantial killing of Palestinian

---

402. I.C.R.C. Press Release No. 1450, Sept. 18, 1982.
403. *Supra* note 354.
404. 75 U.N.T.S. 287, Schindler & Toman, *supra* note 171 at 427.
405. *MacBride Comm.* 163.
406. *Black's Law Dictionary* 727 (rev. 5th ed. 1979).
407. *Id.* at 284.
408. *Id.*

civilians, to enter the camps.[409] In the words of Defense Minister Sharon, the intended role of these units was to "comb out and mop up terrorists."[410] In testimony before the Israeli Commission of Inquiry[411] investigating responsibility for the massacre, Defense Minister Sharon was quoted as stating:

> "I want today, in my name and on behalf of the entire defense establishment, to say that no one foresaw—nor could have foreseen—the atrocities committed in the neighborhoods of Sabra and Shatila."[412]
>
> "No one even imagined or spoke of or worried about this [a massacre], and I begin with myself."[413]

He also testified that he had "anticipated civilian casualties" but not on the mass basis that actually took place.[414] In addition, he claimed that he first learned of "widespread civilian casualties in the refugee camps" at about 9 p.m. on Friday, September 17,[415] which was about 24 hours after the Phalangist militia had entered the camps. He stated that at the same time he learned that Lieutenant General Rafael Eitan, the Chief of Staff, and Major General Amir Drori, the northern area field commander, had ordered the Phalangists to leave the camps by 5 a.m. the next morning and that he considered this a "reasonable" amount of time.[416] Eyewitness accounts stated that most of the killings took place Friday night and Saturday morning after the order to halt the operation had been given.[417] No reasons have been advanced for the delay of several hours after the killings were known to have started other than that it was a "reasonable" time.

According to a report in the Washington Post on September 20, 1982, the radio station of the Israel Defense Force (IDF) announced early on Friday, September 17 that it had been decided on the previous day to send the Phalangist militia into the Beirut refugee camps to carry out "purging operations."[418] The British Broadcasting Corporation monitored the broadcast by IDF correspondent, Arad Mir, and quoted him as saying:

> "The intention is that the IDF will not operate tonight to purge the areas of Sabra and Shatila and the nearby refugee camps."

---

409. The decision was made by the Prime Minister, the Minister of Defense and the Chief of Staff. *Kahan Report* 13. The *Kahan Report* is cited fully in note 413 *infra*. Re known militia hatred of Palestinians, see *supra* note 395. See also *MacBride Comm.* 179-80.

410. *Supra* note 397 at p. A21, col. 3.

411.   The Sept. 19 Cabinet meeting produced a defiant statement charging that it was a "blood libel" to suggest that Israel had any responsibility for the massacre. Ten days later, under intense domestic and international pressure, Begin agreed to the creation of the inquiry board.

Edward Walsh, "Begin Tells Probe Phalangist Killings Weren't Expected," Wash. Post, Nov. 9, 1982, p. A1, col. 5, cont. p. A12, cols. 1-4, at cols. 3-4.

412. Wash. Post, Oct. 26, 1982, p. A1, col. 5, cont. p. A13, cols. 1-5, at p. A1, col. 5.

413. *Id.* at p. A13, col. 4. *The Commission of Inquiry into the Events at the Refugee Camps in Beirut: Final Report* (Authorized Transl., 1983) (hereafter cited as *Kahan Report*) summarizes this statement of Sharon at 44 and 67. The Commission was composed of President of the Supreme Court Yitzak Kahan, Justice of the Supreme Court Aharon Barak, and Major General (Res.) Yona Efrat.

414. Wash. Post, *supra* note 412 at p. A1, col. 5.

415. *Id.* at p. A13, col. 1.

416. *Id.* at col. 2.

417. *Id.*

418. Wash. Post, Sept. 21, 1982, p. A14, col. 6.

"It was decided to entrust the Phalanges with the mission to carry out these purging operations."

"The IDF today completed the encirclement of West Beirut. The forces are now controlling all the main crossroads and roads in the city, and only houses inside the various neighborhoods remain to be purged."[419]

The International Commission summarized Israeli participation in the massacre:

> The Israeli media exposed the following: the militias passed through the Israeli lines on the west side of the camps; IDF-Phalange radio contact continued throughout the operation; the IDF supplied the Phalangists with maps of the camps; the IDF assisted with flares and, within hours of the entry of the Phalange, Israeli HQ was informed that the operation was proceeding in a way inconsistent with the IDF's declared guidelines and alleged purposes.[420]

Additional evidence of Israeli participation from which intent may be inferred was supplied in the testimony before the Israeli Commission of Inquiry on November 7 by Brigadier General Amos Yaron who was the commander of all Israeli forces in the Beirut area and whose immediate superior was Major General Drori.[421] The main points of General Yaron's public testimony have been summarized by Mr. Edward Walsh in the Washington Post:

> Despite reports of civilian casualties, the Israeli Army allowed Lebanese Christian militia units in the Sabra and Shatila refugee camps of West Beirut to bring in fresh troops and restock their ammunition supplies during the second day of the massacre, a senior Israeli Army officer said today.
>
> Brig. Gen. Amos Yaron, the commander of all Israeli forces in the Beirut area, said he authorized the resupply and troop rotation operation even after he and a superior, Maj. Gen. Amir Drori, had become uneasy about the militiamen's behavior and initially had ordered a halt to the militia units' activities in the camps.[422]

The Israeli Commission of Inquiry found that after

> it became known to Brigadier General Yaron [late on Thursday, September 16] that the Phalangists were perpetrating acts of killing which went beyond combat operations, and were killing women and children as well,...he was satisfied with reiterating the warning to the Phalangists' liaison officer and to Elie Hobeika not to kill women and children; but beyond that he did nothing to stop the killing.[423]

The legal significance of this finding is that it provides additional factual basis indicating Israeli complicity which would be a punishable offense under article 3(e) of the Genocide Convention.

Israeli tactical assistance facilitating the massacre is further indicated by their providing illumination for the Phalange units, as described by Edward Walsh in the Washington Post on September 26:

> Thursday evening, the Phalange units began entering the refugee centers under the illumination provided by flares fired from Israeli mortars and dropped from Israeli planes. According to a report by Michael Elkins of the British Broadcasting Corp., Phalangist commanders were in radio contact with Israeli liaison officers outside the camps "and called in a request for flares."

---

419. *Id.*
420. *MacBride Comm.* 173.
421. Wash. Post, Nov. 8, 1982, p. A1, col. 5, cont. p. A17, cols. 4-6.
422. *Id.* at p. A1, col. 5.
423. *Kahan Report, supra* note 413 at 93.

A short time later later, Israeli soldiers on the ground began to encounter hysterical Palestinian women running from the refugee neighborhoods and telling of a massacre going on inside. These accounts were relayed to officers and presumably transmitted along the chain of command.[424]

The danger to Palestinian civilians after the departure of Palestinian combatants was foreseen by all parties involved. Don Oberdorfer reported in the Washington Post on July 11, 1982 that in the negotiations leading to the withdrawal of the combatants the PLO "made involvement of an international force one of its negotiating demands."[425] He also stated that "the PLO is concerned about their family members' security as well as that of many thousands of other Palestinian civilians after the guerrillas departure."[426] The likelihood of danger to the Palestinian civilians was taken into consideration during the negotiations for the PLO departure, and it was dealt with in the ensuing agreement of August 19, 1982 between Lebanon, the United States, France, Italy, Israel, and the PLO.[427] As set forth in this agreement, entitled "Plan for the Departure from Lebanon of the PLO Leadership, Offices and Combatants in Beirut," the United States provided guarantees concerning the "Palestinian noncombatants left behind in Beirut, including the families of those who have departed." The guarantee stated:

> The United States will provide its guarantees on the basis of assurances received from the Government of Israel and from the leadership of certain Lebanese groups with which it has been in touch.[428]

The Lebanese Government also provided guarantees "on the basis of having secured assurance from armed groups with which it has been in touch."[429]

The testimony of Major General Drori before the Israeli Commission, as reported in the Washington Post on November 1, 1982, demonstrates that some Israelis were also concerned about the danger to Palestinian civilians. He stated:

> [H]e and other Israeli officers privately feared that mass killing of civilians would result from the decision to send Lebanese Christian Phalangist militia units into the Palestinian refugee camps of West Beirut.[430]

Given these facts, it is difficult to believe that the Israeli authorities were not aware of the probability of a massacre of Palestinian civilians when they sent in the Phalange militia. If intent is to be inferred from circumstances, and constructive intent exists where one should have reasonably expected or anticipated a particular result, there are plausible grounds for accusations of genocide against those Israeli officials who fall into the Genocide Convention categories in article 3(b), conspiracy to commit genocide, and (c), complicity in genocide. The Report of the International Commission states:

---

424. *Supra* note 397 at p. A22, col. 1.
425. Wash. Post, July 11, 1982, p. A24, cols. 1-2 at col. 1.
426. *Id.*
427. The Agreement is cited in *supra* note 396.
428. *Id.* at art. 4(3).
429. *Id.* at art. 4(2).
430. Edward Walsh, "Israeli Says He Feared Massacre: General's Testimony Conflicts With Sharon's," Wash. Post, Nov. 1, 1982, p. A1, col. 5, cont. p. A19, cols. 1-3 at p. A1, col. 5. *Kahan Report* states at p. 90 that Gen. Drori's knowledge of the Phalange "based on his constant contact with them" showed that he was aware that "the Phalangists were liable to act in an uncontrolled way." See also *MacBride Comm.* 172-79.

79

The massacres that took place at Sabra and Chatila in September 1982 can be described as genocidal massacres, and the term 'complicity in genocide' is wide enough to establish the responsibility of Israel for these acts.[431]

In addition to the basic responsibility of the belligerent occupant under Hague Convention IV[432] and the Civilians Convention,[433] there is individual criminal responsibility for the Phalange perpetrators and those who acted in complicity with them under article 4 of the Genocide Convention.[434] Both Israel and Lebanon, as state-parties to this Convention, were required to enact legislation "to provide effective penalties for persons guilty of genocide or any of the other acts enumerated in article 3."[435] Such persons are to be tried by either a competent domestic tribunal or by an agreed upon international penal tribunal.[436]

F. Grave Breaches of the Civilians Convention

Even if it is determined that the facts do not show commission of the crime of genocide, it is clear that killings have taken place which must be appraised under the grave breaches provisions of the 1949 Civilians Convention. Articles 146 to 148 of this Convention are analagous to the grave breaches provisions of the P.O.W. Convention[437] but are directed specifically to the dangers faced by civilians.

Article 146, like article 129 of the P.O.W. Convention, requires state-parties to enact necessary legislation "to provide effective penal sanctions for persons committing, or ordering to be committed," any of the grave breaches as defined by article 147. Article 146 also requires state-parties to bring such persons to trial. Article 147 defines grave breaches and provides in full:

> Grave breaches to which the preceding Article relates shall be those involving any of the following acts, if committed against persons or property protected by the present Convention: wilful killing, torture or inhuman treatment, including biological experiments, wilfully causing great suffering or serious injury to body or health, unlawful deportation or transfer or unlawful confinement of a protected person, compelling a protected person to serve in the forces of a hostile Power, or wilfully depriving a protected person of the rights of fair and regular trial prescribed in the present Convention, taking of hostages and extensive destruction and appropriation of property, not justified by military necessity and carried out unlawfully and wantonly.

Article 148 is identical to article 131 of the P.O.W. Convention and it codifies the customary law principle of state financial responsibility for violations of law and applies it specifically to violations of article 147 by state-parties to the Conventions. In the context of the protection of civilians, article 148

---

431. "Majority Note on Genocide and Ethnocide," *MacBride Comm.* 194 at 196.
432. *Supra* note 354.
433. *Supra* note 404.
434. *Supra* note 388.
435. *Id.* at art. 5.
436. *Id.* at art. 6.
437. Arts. 129-131. Protocol Additional to the Geneva Conventions of 12 August 1949 and Relating to the Protection of Victims of International Armed Conflicts (Protocol I) of 8 June 1977, Schindler & Toman, *supra* note 171 at 551, contains arts. 11, 85 and 86 concerning grave breaches which are supplementary to those in the Geneva Conventions. Protocol I contains considerable customary law which binds Israel although it is not a party to the Protocol.

should be considered along with article 29 of the Civilians Convention which provides in full:

> The Party to the conflict in whose hands protected persons may be, is responsible for the treatment accorded to them by its agents, irrespective of any individual responsibility which may be incurred.

It is significant that article 29 places obligations upon parties to the conflict rather than only upon state-parties and is not limited to situations involving grave breaches. The grave breaches provisions are supplemented by article 149, common to all the Conventions,[438] which provides for an inter-governmental fact-finding inquiry to be initiated by the state-parties.

Although no such inter-governmental inquiry has been instituted, the International Commission chaired by Sean MacBride has issued a report following a careful investigation of the facts.[439] In addition, under intense internal and international pressure, the Israeli Cabinet on September 28 asked for the establishment of a Commission of Inquiry in accordance with the 1968 domestic Commissions of Inquiry Law,[440] and the Commission was established, with Justice Kahan as chairman, to examine the facts concerning responsibility for the massacres at Sabra and Shatila refugee camps.[441]

The Israeli Commission's Final Report makes a sharp distinction between "direct responsibility" which it placed upon the Phalange, and the "indirect responsibility" of the Israeli political and military leadership. [442] The evidence presented established the danger, and even the probability, of a massacre of the Palestinian civilians in the camps.[443] Because of this, the Commission determined that what actually happened was foreseeable and that the Israeli leadership was indirectly responsible even if it did not intend the result "and merely disregarded the anticipated danger."[444] The Israeli Commission is to be commended for placing at least this limited, or "indirect" responsibility on the Israeli political and military leadership. At the political level, the principal blame was placed upon Minister of Defense Sharon and the Commission found that he bears personal responsibility for not taking necessary steps to avert the foreseen danger and to terminate the massacre.[445] They also found the Chief of Staff, Lieutenant General Eitan,[446] and Major General Drori[447] and Brigadier General Yaron[448] were guilty of not foreseeing the danger and not acting to terminate the killings once they had started.

The Commission's only reference to the applicable international law was its refusal to determine that parts of Lebanon, including West Beirut and the refugee camps, were occupied territory according to the criteria of international law[449] in spite of the common article 2 of the four Geneva Conventions for the

---

438. Conv. I, art. 52; Conv. II, art. 53; Conv. III, art. 132.
439. A full citation to the MacBride Comm. Report is in *supra* note 252.
440. *Kahan Report* 1. The statute is in 23 Israel Laws (auth. transl.) 32 (1968).
441. A full citation to the Kahan Comm. Report is in *supra* note 413.
442. *Kahan Report* 48.
443. *Id.* at 27, 60, 67-69, and *passim*.
444. *Id.* at 54-60.
445. *Id.* at 67-71.
446. *Id.* at 74-80.
447. *Id.* at 89-92.
448. *Id.* at 93-96.
449. *Id.* at 54.

Protection of War Victims which specifies that each Convention "shall also apply to all cases of partial or total occupation of the territory of a High Contracting Party." In addition, article 29 of the Civilians Convention established the responsibility of the occupying power for treatment accorded to protected persons by its agents. It is clear that the Palestinian civilians in the Sabra and Shatila camps were protected persons within the meaning of the Geneva Civilians Convention.[450] The evidence before the Commission which is referred to repeatedly in its Report establishes that the Phalange was not merely an agent of the Government of Israel in some generalized sense, but that it was under IDF command control.[451] Even if there had been only a loose agency relationship between the Government of Israel and the Phalange, the Government of Israel would still be responsible for the maintenance of public order and safety as the belligerent occupant under the basic principles of international law.[452]

The Commission's findings cannot be regarded as complying with the grave breaches requirements of the Civilians Convention. No inquiry was made concerning the extent to which the facts brought out by the testimony before the Commission concerning IDF command control and the provision of support and assistance throughout the massacre constituted responsibility for any of the specifically enumerated grave breaches in article 147. Even if it should be contended that Israel has a statute which meets the requirements of article 146 by providing penal sanctions for persons "ordering to be committed" the specified grave breaches, the Commission made no suggestion that appropriate criminal prosecutions be undertaken. Such prosecution should not only involve the Israeli military personnel whom the Commission found to be "indirectly responsible," but also the officers and members of the Phalange militia who participated in the massacre.

The Government of Lebanon has initiated an inquiry which appears to be only *pro forma*. It has thus far produced no known findings and is not expected to produce any significant ones because of the reported links between the Phalangist movement and some elements in the Government of Lebanon.[453]

In addition to the criminal liabilities of individuals, the Civilians Convention specifies further responsibilities. Under article 148, state-parties are responsible for grave breaches committed in violation of article 147. In the situation of occupied territory, the responsible party is the belligerent occupant rather than the sovereign. Since Lebanon was only the nominal sovereign where the massacre took place, it would have at most a secondary responsibility for what occurred. Because the Sabra and Shatila camps were within the area of Beirut occupied by the Israeli Army at the time of the massacre, the Government of Israel had the primary legal responsibility.

There is also a serious question of the responsibility of the United States Government. The agreement concerning the departure of PLO combatants

---

450. See *MacBride Comm.* at 163.
451. *Kahan Report* 8, 10, 20, 24, and *passim*. From time to time, but not during the massacre, the Phalange was directed by the Israeli Mossad [Institute for Intelligence and Special Projects]. *Id.* at 7-8.
452. Hague Conv. IV, Annexed Regs., *supra* note 175, art. 43.
453. Loren Jenkins, "In Lebanon, Massacre is Hushed Up," Wash. Post, Dec. 24, 1982, p. A1, cols. 4-6, cont. p. A8, cols. 1-4.

from Beirut of August 19, 1982[454] was designed, *inter alia*, to prevent the commission of crimes which would constitute grave breaches as defined in article 147. If the agreement had been honored, the massacre would not have taken place. In the agreement the United States provided its "guarantees," *inter alia*, on the basis of "assurances" received from the Government of Israel.[455] In the letter from Ambassador Habib, the Personal Representative of the President of the United States, to the Prime Minister of Lebanon (to avoid the appearance of communicating directly to the PLO) it was stated.

> I would also like to assure you that the United States government fully recognizes the importance of these assurances from the government of Israel and that my government will do its utmost to ensure that these assurances are scrupulously observed.[456]

There is at least reasonable doubt as to whether the protests which were made over the Israeli entrance into West Beirut constitute compliance with the undertakings made by the United States.[457]

The protection of civilians on a nondiscriminatory basis is dependent upon the implementation of the existing sanctions provisions of the applicable international conventions. The failure to invoke these sanctions in the case of particular grave breaches can become a precedent for further destruction of civilian human and material values.

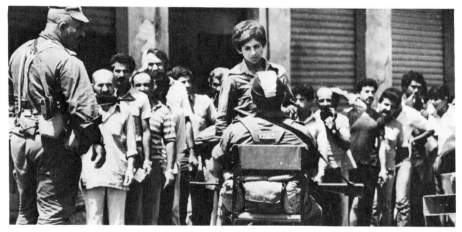

Wide World Photos

Israeli border guards interrogate Arab men near Sidon on July 19, 1982. Thousands of men suspected of armed activity were detained in a nearby camp after roundups like this one.

454. *Supra* note 396.
455. The negotiating history of the Agreement of Aug. 19, 1982 which demonstrates clearly the United States undertaking in four documents to guarantee "the 'security of the camps' where Palestinian civilians lived" is set forth in the Wash. Post, Nov. 13, 1982, p. A1, col. 6, cont. p. A14, cols. 1-3, and p. A15, cols. 1-3.
456. M. Viorst, "America's Broken Pledge to the PLO," Wash. Post, Dec. 19, 1982, p. C1, cols. 1-5, cont. p. C2, cols. 1-6, at col. 1.
457. See the reports of United States official knowledge when the massacre was taking place in W. Blitzer, "Officials Say U.S. Had Early Word of Massacre," Jerusalem Post, Int'l Ed., Feb. 6-12, 1983, p. 10, cols. 4-5. See the appraisal of the Israeli move into West Beirut in J.C. Harsch, "A Trail of Deceit," Christian Sci. Monitor, Sept. 28, 1982, p. 22, col. 1.

IV. Appraisal of the Role of the United States Secretary of State in the Israeli June, 1982 Attack-Invasion

Former Secretary of State Alexander M. Haig, Jr. has written a book, *Caveat: Realism, Reagan, and Foreign Policy,*[458] which tells about his own role and that of President Reagan during Haig's tenure as Secretary of State. The President appears as an affable figure acting, on more than one occasion, on the advice provided by the person who talked to him immediately prior to a decision being made. Secretary Haig writes, with a tone of apology, that his own "frankness may startle."[459] Anyone who is concerned with the relationship between international and domestic law and foreign policy, however, can only appreciate his candor.

On occasion Haig reveals himself as a person who understands the centrality of human values and can express compassion when they are denied. For example, in referring to the situation in El Salvador he says: "No one could be unmoved by such a spectacle of poverty and social injustice and cultural deprivation."[460] Describing the situation in Poland caused by the rise of the Solidarity labor movement and governmental repression, he writes: "Bloodshed was a clear possibility. Above all, we must do nothing that might lay us open to a charge of triggering it."[461]

In the penultimate chapter on Lebanon,[462] Secretary Haig sets forth certain matters of assumed facts, reveals his predispositions on the events which transpired, and recounts the decisions which were made.

A. Statements of Assumed Facts

In his chapter on the attack-invasion Haig states as a fact a view which was constantly reiterated by Israeli officials, including Ambassador Blum in the Security Council.[463] Referring to the situation following the Israeli-Palestinian Cease-Fire Agreement of July 24, 1981, arranged by the United States and Saudi Arabia, Haig writes:

> For more than a year, Israel, goaded by the bombardment of her northern settlements by Palestinian gunners from fortified sanctuaries in southern Lebanon and by terrorist attacks on her citizens at home and abroad, had wanted to send her ground forces into Lebanon and destroy the PLO.[464]

---

458. Macmillan, New York (1984) [hereafter cited as Haig]..
459. Haig 358.
460. *Id.* 117.
461. *Id.* 250.
462. *Id.* 317-52.
463. See the similar Blum statement in the text accompanying *supra* note 92.
464. Haig 317. No attempt is made by the authors to consider all of Haig's assumed facts.

This statement is inaccurate in several respects. It is contrary to the careful, and undisputed, reports of Lieutenant-General Callaghan, the commander of the United Nations Interim Force in Lebanon (UNIFIL), considered previously.[465] The Callaghan reports document the opposite: Repeated Israeli land, sea and air violations of the July 24, 1981 Agreement and only one limited Palestine Liberation Organization (PLO) response to the continual provocations.[466] In fairness to Haig, he does not explicitly state that the "terrorist attacks" were carried out by the PLO. This statement, however, is the first of many indications that Haig either does not understand or prefers not to mention that Israeli claims were not limited to "citizens" but applied to the alleged constituency of "the Jewish people" consisting of "Jews" wherever located.[467]

The next statement of "fact" is that:

The primary obstacle to peace in Lebanon had been the presence of two foreign armies—the Syrian "peacekeeping" force and the military arm of the PLO.... [468]

He is apparently unaware that ever since the March, 1978 invasion the Israeli Defense Forces (IDF) have remained in Lebanon either directly or through the Haddad militia, armed, trained, and paid by Israel. He adds elsewhere that "the Israelis invaded the south briefly in 1978."[469]

Secretary Haig states flatly that the Camp David Agreements are "the only existing mechanism capable of advancing toward the solution of the wider Arab-Israeli conflict and the Palestinian question."[470] He ignores the two-state solution under law proposed by the United Nations with the support of virtually the entire world community except the United States and Israel.[471]

In Haig's view, "Lebanon's population of about 3 million is almost evenly divided between Muslims and Christians."[472] In fact it is commonly accepted that within Lebanon, Muslims substantially outnumber Christians.[473] This is the cause of opposition by the Christian elite to a census or a democratic sharing of power. Even the most junior area specialist in the Department of State, if asked, could have corrected the Secretary of State's error on this matter. Haig has written, however, that: "The State [Department's] foreign policy bureaucracy,

465. See the text accompanying *supra* notes 45-54.
466. *Id.*
467. See the text accompanying *supra* notes 35-37, 114-115.
468. Haig 318.
469. *Id.* 321.
470. *Id.* 320.
471. See W.T. Mallison, "The United Nations and the National Rights of the People of Palestine" in *Palestinian Rights: Affirmation and Denial* 25 (I. Abu-Lughod, ed., 1982).
472. Haig 320.
473. See, *e.g.,* Faksh, "Lebanon: The Road to Disintegration," *American-Arab Affairs* No. 8, p. 20 at 22 (Spring 1984) where reference is made to the higher Muslim birth rate and the reluctance of the Christian elite to recognize the contemporary demographic reality.

[was] overwhelmingly Arabist in its approach to the Middle East and in its sympathies...."[474]

Describing events after the Israeli-PLO Agreement of July 24, 1981, Haig writes:

> Since the cessation of hostilities slightly more than six months before, Israel had lost 17 dead and 288 wounded in ten PLO violations.[475]

This statement is very similar to the factually inaccurate statement that Ambassador Blum made to the Security Council on June 6, 1982, except that the alleged figures of dead and wounded are stated by Haig to be accurate as of February, 1982. The Haig statement is false for the same reason that the Blum statement, quoted earlier, is false.[476] Like Blum, Haig assumes PLO involvement without providing any supporting evidence. Like Blum, he also assumes that the July 24, 1981 Cease-Fire Agreement applied world-wide, although he admits elsewhere that this is inconsistent with its terms.[477] Like Blum, Haig does not refer to the much larger number of Palestinians killed by Israeli armed forces or by Zionist settlers armed and supported by the Government of Israel during the interval between the Agreement of July 24, 1981 and the Israeli attack-invasion.[478]

In summary, Haig takes unsubstantiated official Israeli propaganda statements as the basis for his understanding of the fact situation in the time between the July 24, 1981 Agreement and the Israeli attack-invasion less than a year later. This presents a striking contrast to his understanding of other conflict situations. The chapter on the Falklands/Malvinas crisis[479] and the ensuing armed conflict reveals Haig as having an accurate understanding of the fact situation and the contrasting, and indeed ultimately incompatible, British and Argentinian positions. There Haig demonstrated by words and actions his deep commitment to a peaceful solution. From the outset he viewed "the right indisputably" on the British side.[480] He writes that he went to London to assure Prime Minister Thatcher "that she had the support of the United States in a right course of action."[481]

B. Predispositions and Decisions Leading to the Attack-Invasion

Secretary Haig is commendably candid in his revelations concerning his predispositions and decisions. Both were based to a large extent upon his failure to understand the existing facts prior to the attack-invasion. His predispositions

---

474. Haig 334. Haig was deeply concerned that both the "bureaucracy" (*id.*) and the British Foreign Minister, Lord Carrington, (*id.* at 327) wanted to bring the PLO into the peace process.
475. *Id.* 332.
476. See the text accompanying *supra* notes 110–118.
477. Haig 332.
478. See the text accompanying *supra* notes 130-135.
479. Haig 261-302.
480. *Id.* 272.
481. *Id.* 273.

reveal a different mind-set from that described in earlier chapters and deserve separate treatment along with his ensuing decisions.

His assumptions concerning then Israeli Prime Minister Menachem Begin provide an appropriate starting place. In Haig's view: "Begin is a lawyer, absorbed in legalism, detail, and nuance...."[482] Begin won "respect" because of, *inter alia*, "the force of his character."[483] Begin's views on the Israeli settlements in the occupied territories (that he made no promise to stop further settlements permanently as part of the Camp David Agreements) are set forth with deference.[484] Former President Carter's inconsistent understanding is not mentioned. On another issue, Haig writes that "it was fruitless to question his [Begin's] basic assumptions."[485] In Haig's view, Begin could be "combative" or "harsh" but "he is scrupulously truthful."[486]

Haig admits to several "surprises" from the Government of Israel. He refers to the Israeli attack on the Iraqi reactor on June 7, 1981 as "a startling and dangerous action" but not "technically an attack on a peaceful nation" since Iraq and Israel had been in a "state of war" since 1948.[487] Haig's feelings, however, were "mixed" and he writes that the "suspicion that Iraq intended to produce neclear weapons" was not "unrealistic."[488] Although some of the President's advisers recommended "punitive"[489] measures against Israel, Haig reports his own position was that "our strategic interests would not be served by policies that humiliated and weakened Israel."[490]

---

482. *Id.* 322.
483. *Id.*
484. *Id.* 326.
485. *Id.* 186.
486. Haig does not mention Begin's and Sharon's less recent apparent criminal activities. Begin is probably best known for the massacre of Palestinian villagers at Deir Yassin. See the account by Jacques de Reynier [then International Committee of the Red Cross Delegate for Palestine], *A Jerusalem un drapeau flottait sur la ligne de feu* 69–74 (Neuchâtel, 1950). Sharon is probably best known for his command of Unit 101 of the Israeli Army, which like the Nazi Einsatzgruppen, was trained and used to kill civilians. See D. Hirst, *The Gun and the Olive Branch: The Roots of Violence in the Middle East* (1977) under index headings "Unit 101" and "Sharon." See also several volumes of the State Department's official *Foreign Relations of the United States*. See, *e.g.* [1947] *id.*, Vol. 5 (1971) under general index heading "Palestine" and specific headings "Irgun Zvai Leumi," "Jewish Agency for Palestine," "Stern Gang" and "Terrorism." As recently as a few years ago a complete set of *Foreign Relations of the U.S.* was kept in the Office of the Secretary of State.
487. Haig 183. Haig is apparently unaware of the contemporary irrelevance of the so-called technical "state of war." See Mallison & Mallison, "The Israeli Aerial Attack of June 7, 1981 Upon the Iraqi Nuclear Reactor: Aggression or Self-Defense?", 15 *Vanderbilt J. Transnational L.* 417 at 432-34 (1982).
488. Haig 184. Secretary Haig does not mention Israel's nuclear weapons capability which it had achieved some years ago. See Mallison & Mallison, *supra* note 487 at note 113 and accompanying text.
489. Haig 184.
490. *Id.*

Israel's annexation of the Golan Heights of Syria on December 14, 1981, he admits, was an "astonishing act" which "inflamed" Israel's critics in the Administration.[491] The President decided the "cost" would be suspension of the two-week-old U.S.-Israeli Memorandum of Understanding establishing limited strategic cooperation.[492] This "provoked a memorable outburst" from Begin to U.S. Ambassador to Israel Samuel W. Lewis,[493] which Haig quotes at some length and without comment: "What kind of talk is this—'penalizing' Israel?" Begin, "livid with anger," continued, "Are we a state or [are we] vassals of yours? Are we a banana republic?...You have no right to penalize Israel."[494] U.S. Government reaction is not mentioned.

At President Sadat's funeral in October, 1981, Begin informed the Secretary of State that if the changed Egyptian situation threatened Israeli interests, Begin's "will" or "freedom" to return the Sinai might disappear.[495] From this, Haig writes, "one could read the reality."[496] When the Sinai was returned on schedule on April 25, 1982, Haig wrote Begin that it was "an act of the utmost courage, statesmanship, and vision...."[497] At this point, in Haig's words, "Israeli fixation on the threat from southern Lebanon intensified."[498] No mention is made of the continuing attacks on Palestinian civilians in the occupied territories and in Lebanon or of the attacks on Lebanese civilians.[499]

It was also at the Sadat funeral that Begin told Haig of an Israeli plan to move into Lebanon, the first time that any Israeli "had been quite so specific."[500] Haig replied:

If you move, you move alone....Unless there is a major, internationally recognized provocation, the United States will not support such an action.[501]

As the subject arose "again and again" in subsequent months, Haig reports that President Reagan and he always responded that "an internationally recognized provocation"[502] would be required and sometimes added that the "response must be proportionate."[503] Nevertheless, Haig "never believed that mere words would restrain Israel...."[504] In early 1982, Begin, in "his lawyerly fashion"

---

491. *Id.* 328.
492. *Id.* Formal U.S.-Israeli strategic cooperation was revived in late 1983. See M. Hameed, "The Impact and Implications of the U.S.-Israeli Strategic Cooperation Agreement," *American-Arab Affairs,* No. 8, p. 13 (Spring, 1984).
493. Haig 329.
494. Each of the Begin words quoted appears at *id.*
495. *Id.* 326.
496. *Id.*
497. *Id.* 330.
498. *Id.*
499. See the text accompanying *supra* notes 130-135 re the Israeli killings of civilians.
500. Haig 326.
501. *Id.*
502. *Id.* 327 and *passim.*
503. *E.g., id.* 335.
504. *Id.* 330.

attempted "to redefine the conditions under which the United States would consider an Israeli attack justified."[505] Haig repeated his standard formula, adding the requirement of proportionality in response.[506] Haig writes:

> Begin agreed, then changed his mind, and in one of his exercises in creative nuance, told Reagan that there would be no major Israeli action "unless [Israel was] attacked in clear provocation."[507]

There is no indication that Haig rejected the redefinition.

Changes in the stated position of the Government of Israel, as well as its "surprising" actions, were viewed by Haig with equanimity. In contrast, during events leading up to the armed conflict in the Falklands/Malvinas, he was frustrated and outraged by changes in the Argentinian position. He describes them as a "blatant double-cross"[508] and evidence of "bad faith...unique in my experience as a negotiator."[509]

In March and April, 1982, Haig reports, "the storm continued to gather."[510] He writes, in a matter of fact tone:

> An Israeli diplomat was assassinated in Paris, and an Israeli officer was killed in the Haddad enclave. Israeli planes attacked PLO targets in Lebanon on April 21 and again on May 9...."[511]

There is no suggestion that the events described provided either a reasonable or lawful basis for Israeli attacks on "PLO targets," Palestinian refugee camps, and Lebanese villagers.

Haig reports that he attempted unsuccessful diplomatic measures which were intended, *inter alia,* to "perhaps even help to bring the Syrians and the PLO to their senses."[512] In this frame of mind he received a late May visit from "General Sharon" (the Israeli Defense Minister) who "shocked" State Department "bureaucrats" by sketching out two alternative possible military incursions into Lebanon.[513] Haig challenged these plans in the group meeting and then, for emphasis, repeated his formula to Sharon in private.[514] Sharon had the last unchallenged word:

> "No one," Sharon replied, in his truculent way, "has the right to tell Israel what decision it should take in defense of its people."[515]

---

505. *Id.* 332.
506. *Id.*
507. *Id.*
508. *Id.* 283.
509. *Id.* 290.
510. *Id.* 333.
511. *Id.*
512. *Id.* 334.
513. *Id.* 335.
514. *Id.*
515. *Id.* Sharon's quoted position of unilateral decision not subject to review is identical with that of Nazi defendants convicted by the I.M.T. See the text accompanying *supra* note 126.

The Israeli investigative reporter, Mr. Ze'ev Schiff, wrote of United States acquiescence or consent to the forthcoming attack-invasion in an article entitled "The Green Light" published in 1983.[516] He wrote that the suspension of the Memorandum of Understanding on strategic cooperation deprived Defense Minister Sharon of the cover for his planned moves into Lebanon. A new rationale, therefore, was required.[517] Schiff's account of the May meeting between Sharon and Haig is strikingly similar to Haig's later published account.[518] Schiff points out that Sharon noted carefully that Haig made no threat against the forthcoming military action[519] and that Haig:

> emphasized that it would take an unquestionable breach of the cease-fire by the PLO to warrant an Israeli riposte.[520]

Schiff adds that the "halfhearted, feeble warnings subsequently voiced by Haig were irrelevant"[521] and that after Haig's response was reported to Begin, no Israeli minister was in a position to oppose the move against the PLO and Lebanon.[522]

Schiff writes that the "pretext" came sooner than Washington thought it would.[523] The event was the attack on the Israeli ambassador in London on June 3. Schiff reports: "No one in the Israeli cabinet bothered to check whether the assailants were actually PLO members."[524]

Haig writes that the *"casus belli"* which "the Israelis had been waiting for" occurred on June 3.[525] Here Haig uses Latin with commendable precision. His term is most accurately translated as occasion or opportunity for war. In contrast, the term *causa belli,* not used by Haig, is translated as a cause or reason for war. It is clear that Haig thought the first term properly complied with his inadequate "warnings" to the Israelis.

Haig's description of the June 3 *"casus belli"* is that the perpetrators were "Arab terrorists."[526] He is either unaware or prefers not to mention that the British Government had identified the assailants as members of an anti-PLO

---

516. *Foreign Policy* No. 50, p. 73 (Spring, 1983).
517. *Id.* 78.
518. *Id.* 80.
519. *Id.* 80-81.
520. *Id.* 81.
521. *Id.*
522. *Id.*
523. *Id.* 82.
524. *Id.* As the Second Edition of the present book is going to press, a new book, Ze'ev Schiff & Ehud Yaari, *Israel's Lebanon War* (Simon & Schuster, New York, 1984) has just been published. It provides further evidence of Secretary Haig's complicity in the attack-invasion.
525. Haig 335.
526. *Id.*

gang.[527] In addition, Haig should have been aware that the June 3 attack on the Israeli ambassador, like others claimed by the Government of Israel, was not a violation of the June 24, 1981 Cease-Fire Agreement. Even if the June 3 attempt to kill Ambassador Argov had been carried out by PLO members acting on the instructions of the PLO leadership, it could not, under the criteria of international law agreed to by civilized states, amount to either an armed attack or an anticipated armed attack upon the State of Israel.[528] Upon his recovery, Ambassador Argov denounced his government in unequivocal terms for the pretext it had employed to start the attack-invasion.[529]

Haig reports that the Saudis informed him on or about June 5 that the PLO was willing to stop responding fire.[530] In Haig's view it was "too late" to stop the attack-invasion because "Begin's deepest emotions had been engaged."[531] No mention is made of the contemporary report of the Secretary-General that the PLO, like Lebanon and unlike Israel, had agreed to and carried out the cease-fire demanded of all parties in Security Council resolution 508 of June 5, 1982.[532] The important matter, which is implicit in Haig's account, is that the Government of Israel and the Government of the United States, acting through Secretary of State Haig, had their *"casus belli"* and the attack-invasion was started.

Among the most obvious and depressing conclusions which strike the reader of Haig's chapter on the June, 1982 attack-invasion is that of the professional incompetence of a Secretary of State who is unable or unwilling to ascertain a reasonably accurate factual understanding of crucial events and participants in spite of the comprehensive informational and intelligence sources available to him through the Department of State and other agencies of the United States Government. His failure to use available resources here is in striking contrast to his stated intention when he undertook to serve as Secretary of State:

> I wanted a strong ring of professionals around me in key jobs. I needed their experience and their competence.[533]

Another such obvious conclusion is the manifest prejudice of a Secretary of State who listens almost exclusively to, and is easily persuaded by, one partisan

---

527. See *supra* note 58 and accompanying text.
   See Dorsey, "Abu Nidal: willing tool for terror," *Middle East Int'l,* No. 228, p. 10 (29 June 1984) for an account of the friendly relationships between Abu Nidal's relatives living in the West Bank and the Israeli occupation regime as well as the view that Abu Nidal's acts of terror have consistently "benefited" Israel.
528. See the text accompanying *supra* note 118.
529. It is possible that some, unlike Ambassador Argov, might wish to cite as a precedent the shooting of a Nazi diplomat in Paris, Ernst vom Rath, by an individual identified by the Nazis as a Jew. This was the pretext used in "justification" for the infamous Nazi attacks on Jews and their property known as "Crystal Night."
530. Haig 336.
531. *Id.*
532. The text accompanying *supra* notes 101-105.
533. Haig 63.

91

participant to a continuing and then intensified conflict situation. The purpose of serious interest in the views of other partisans is not, of course, to be necessarily persuaded by them but rather to reach reasoned as opposed to idiosyncratic policy positions.[534] The degree of prejudice concerning the June, 1982 attack-invasion was such that the non-partisan and factually accurate findings of the Secretary-General of the United Nations, based in substantial part on the unquestioned findings of fact by Lieutenant-General Callaghan, were simply ignored.[535] Both the U.S. Mission to the United Nations and the State Department's Bureau of International Organization Affairs were fully informed even though there is no indication that the information went beyond them.

Throughout his book, Secretary Haig treats President Reagan with deference and even admiration. Unfortunately, Haig's account provides no evidence of competent leadership or even thoughtful decision-making by Reagan. On issues concerning the Middle East in general and the June, 1982 attack-invasion in particular, Reagan's understanding often appears to be on a level with Haig's. The significant constitutional point, however, is that Reagan is fully responsible for Haig's demonstrated incompetence and prejudice because the President, under the U.S. Constitution, has full responsibility for the conduct of foreign affairs. As Chief Justice John Marshall put it long ago: "The President is the sole organ [directly or through his subordinates] of the nation in its external relations, and its sole representative with foreign nations."[536]

It should be mentioned that Haig's humanitarianism does not extend to Palestinian and Lebanese civilians and combatants. In his consideration of the Falklands/Malvinas armed conflict, he writes: "The fighting men on both sides showed bravery and humanitarian feeling for wounded enemies and prisoners."[537] No such sentiments are applied to Palestinian and Lebanese civilians who were the objects of direct military attacks in violation of one of the most elementary principles of humanity and law.[538] There is no evidence of compassion for homeless refugees who have been driven from their homes (for many, more than once) and deprived of their property by a systematic policy of state terror which contin-

---

534. In fairness to Secretary Haig it was Secretary Kissinger who thought of the policy (alleged by some to be an agreement with Israel) of not talking to the PLO except, of course, when some immediate advantage is perceived such as the safe departure of United States nationals from a conflict area. This does not, however, relieve Reagan of responsibility because the Constitution grants the negotiating power to him and if Kissinger has attempted to give, or bargain, it away, the attempted derogation of the Constitution fails and the President still has the negotiating power.

535. See the text accompanying *supra* notes 44-54.

536. Quoted in E.S. Corwin, *The President: Office and Powers* 216 and note 27 (3rd rev. ed. 1948).

537. Haig 295.

538. See the text of *supra* Chap. I, Sec. C and Chap. III, Sec. C to the end of the chapter.

ues to enjoy the tacit and direct support of the United States Government.[539] No mention is made of the barbaric and racially discriminatory treatment of prisoners, both civilian and military and including medical personnel, by their captors.[540]

C. Participation in the Ongoing Attack-Invasion

Perhaps the more obvious ways in which the United States Government participated in the attack-invasion were through military supplies consisting, *inter alia,* of weapons, tanks, aircraft and munitions. Secretary Haig recounts in appropriate detail the diplomatic methods of participation.

Following assurances that operation "Peace for Galilee" involved only a 40-kilometer advance to remove Israeli settlements from the range of PLO artillery,[541] Haig received further "surprises." In addition to the advance far beyond 40 kilometers, Israel attacked and destroyed Syrian surface-to-air missiles. As to the latter, Haig writes, it "is still not clear what prompted this sudden Israeli attack, which changed the whole character of the conflict."[542]

Haig provides a meticulous recounting of Israeli military casualties.[543] Begin had told him of Israel's concern about this subject *prior* to the attack-invasion:

> "We do not worry about victory," Begin had told us before the operation began. "We worry about casualties."[544]

One set of figures recounted by Haig (apparently as of June 11) is 170 Israeli military personnel killed and 700 wounded. On the basis of comparative populations, Haig notes that this would be equivalent "to the United States losing 10,000 dead

---

539. The amount and quality of the U.S. Government and Zionist-Israel documentation on the state terror resulting in the killing or expulsion of the Palestinians is substantial. In addition to various volumes of the *Foreign Relations of the United States,* referred to in *supra* note 486, see *e.g.* Lieutenant-Colonel Netanel Lorch [the head of the Historical Division of the Israeli General Staff during 1947-1949] on "Plan Dalet" which involved concerted attacks on Palestinian civilians throughout Palestine prior to the Israeli unilateral Declaration of the Establishment of the State of Israel on May 14, 1948 in his book, *The Edge of the Sword: Israel's War of Independence, 1947-1949,* p. 87 (1961).

  The *Personal Diary* of Mr. Moshe Sharett (the first foreign minister and the second prime minister of the State of Israel) is the preeminent inside account of the early years of the Israeli state terror. It is available in Israel in Hebrew. L. Rokach, *Israel's Sacred Terrorism: A Study Based on Moshe Sharett's Personal Diary and Other Documents* (Assoc. of Arab-Amer. Univ. Graduates, 1980) provides penetrating analysis in English. See the text accompanying *supra* note 19.
540. See the text accompanying *supra* notes 244-264.
541. Haig 337.
542. *Id.* 338.
543. *Id.* 337, 341, 345.
544. *Id.* 341.

and 40,000 wounded in a week."[545] No comment is made and no figures are provided concerning either Palestinian or Lebanese civilian casualties.

Apparently Haig was not concerned about Security Council resolution 509 of June 6, 1982[546] which had no discernible influence on the massive land invasion which started that day. On June 8 the attack-invasion was progressing according to plan and the Spanish draft resolution of that day[547] presented a major obstacle to him. It differed from earlier resolutions by referring in its fifth operative paragraph to future consideration of "practical ways and means in accordance with the Charter of the United Nations" if hostilities were not terminated within six hours in compliance with resolutions 508 and 509. The word "sanctions" was not mentioned.

Haig learned of Reagan's initial support for the Spanish draft resolution from William P. Clark, the President's National Security Adviser who, when asked as to who had made the decision to support the resolution, responded: "The President of the United States, Al; we've got the decision and there is no more discussion."[548] Clark added that Reagan acted on the recommendation of Vice President Bush's crisis management team.[549] Haig writes: "This would have been an unprecedented step for the United States."[550] He thereby appears to overlook President Eisenhower's position in 1956 and 1957.[551] Haig immediately talked to Reagan:

> I advised him that the United States must veto the resolution not only because it placed the entire blame for hostilities on Israel but also because sanctions were implied.[552]

Reagan changed his mind and with "only minutes to spare" Haig telephoned Mrs. Kirkpatrick to "veto" the resolution without regard to any other instructions she may have received.[553] There was probably no other way in which the United States Government, having previously assented to the starting of the attack-invasion, could indicate so effectively its support for the now changed and expanded military objectives.

---

545. *Id.*
546. The text accompanying *supra* note 141.
547. U.N. Doc. S/15185 in Appendix C.
548. Haig 338.
549. *Id.* 338-39.
550. *Id.* 339.
551. See the text accompanying *infra* notes 595-597.
552. Haig 339.
553. *Id.* All other members of the Security Council voted in favor of the Spanish draft.
    Noam Chomsky, *The Fateful Triangle: The United States, Israel and the Palestinians,* Chap. 5 entitled "Peace for Galilee" (1983), like Secretary Haig, provides persuasive evidence of U.S. Government participation in the planning and carrying out of the June, 1982 attack-invasion. Unlike Haig's, Chomsky's evidence is based upon external rather than internal sources.

On June 10, Haig took another opportunity to prevent possible inhibition of the Israeli political and military leadership. He found that President Reagan had already signed a letter to Begin "calling in harsh terms for an unconditional Israeli withdrawal from Lebanon."[554] Haig wrote:

> I reminded the President that this letter, expressing demands that the Israelis could not possibly meet, gave them justification for inflexibility.[555]

No suggestions were made as to how the Government of Israel could demonstrate further inflexibility. In any event, the President changed his mind again and the letter was not sent.[556]

Haig reports that he encountered difficulties with other members of the administration and that most of the President's advisers, who were "exasperated by Begin's unpredictability" and "outraged by the attack on Lebanon," became "determined to punish Israel."[557] "The President's anger with Begin, fed by the greater anger of Weinberger" appeared to increase "by the day."[558]

Haig's own reaction was quite different from that which he manifested concerning alleged changing Argentine positions during the Falklands/Malvinas crisis.[559] He writes:

> I continually attempted to reassure the President and Clark, by explaining that Israeli pressure, and it alone, could produce a solution that would end the fighting.[560]

Haig emphasized to the President the crucial importance of not clarifying the U.S. Government position publicly. Although Haig deemed it permissible to complain to the Israelis privately he felt that "we don't need a public break with Israel."[561]

He makes much of the opportunity the ongoing conflict provided for the achievement of peace. For example:

> In this tragic situation lay the great opportunity to make peace. Syria and the PLO, the two forces that had destroyed the authority of the Lebanese government and brought on the fighting, had been defeated.[562]

In spite of some difficulties, such as the particularly intense bombardment of Beirut on June 25, which Haig terms "a heavy-handed act,"[563] he believed that, shortly before he left office, "all of the pieces were falling into place."[564]

---

554. Haig 341.
555. *Id.*
556. *Id.*
557. *Id.* 344.
558. *Id.* 345.
559. The text accompanying *supra* notes 508-509.
560. Haig 345.
561. *Id.* 346.
562. *Id.* 342.
563. *Id.* 346.
564. *Id.* 350.

After he left office he was discouraged by the changing United States policy indicated by Secretary of State-designate George Shultz, during his confirmation hearings before the Senate, when "special emphasis" was placed on the "legitimate needs and problems of the Palestinian people."[565]

D. Violations of Law by the United States Government

1. Violation of Domestic Law

The statute concerning the supplying of United States weapons and munitions[566] (termed "Defense articles and defense services") requires that they be provided "solely" for one or more of the following purposes: (1) Internal security; (2) "legitimate self-defense"; (3) regional or collective arrangements or measures consistent with the United Nations Charter or participation in collective measures requested by the United Nations; or (4) to enable the foreign armed forces of recipient states to construct public works or otherwise promote economic and social development. The statute is consistent with the customary and treaty obligations (including the United Nations Charter) of the United States. Secretary Haig has indicated that he may be aware of the existence of the statute. In connection with the June 7, 1981 Israeli attack on the Iraqi nuclear reactor, he writes: "American equipment, delivered to the Israelis for defensive purposes only, had been used in the attack."[567] There is, however, no direct or indirect mention of the statute in connection with the June, 1982 attack-invasion. He also appears to have been aware that the Israeli attack-invasion did not meet the legal requirements of "legitimate self-defense." In his eagerness to "veto" the Spanish draft Security Council resolution of June 8, 1982[568] he indicated that it made no difference to him whether or not Israel was specifically named in the draft since "no other country except Israel could possibly be the object of condemnation and sanctions."[569] Even if he lacked knowledge of the statute, Secretary Haig was, as both a citizen and an officer of the United States, bound by its terms.

President Reagan's suspension of the shipment of cluster bombs to Israel in late July, 1982 did not amount to compliance with the terms of the law.[570] The United States Government throughout the attack-invasion initiated in June, 1982, as well as in the unlawful use of the United States-supplied defense articles before and since then, has violated the law which it is duty bound to uphold.

---

565. *Id.* 351-52.
566. Appendix D.
567. Haig 183.
568. The text accompanying *supra* notes 143 and 547.
569. Haig 339.
570. *Supra* note 369 and accompanying text.
   A secret report from the State Department to Congress on July 16, 1982 concluded "that Israel may have violated U.S. arms agreements during the invasion of Lebanon" according to the Wash. Post, July 17, 1982, p. A12, cols. 1-2. This is as frank an admission of violation of law as could be expected. If there had been no violation the report would not have been secret.

2. Violation of International Law

The basic international law obligations of the United States are set forth in the world legal order which is enunciated in the customary law and in the treaty law including the United Nations Charter.[571] The United States-Israel Mutual Defense Assistance Agreement which has been in effect since July 23, 1952[572] contains restrictive terms which make it technically consistent with the world legal order as well as with the domestic law which has just been considered.[573] The second numbered paragraph of the first of the two diplomatic notes which comprise the agreement sets forth the four requirements of the basic statute with emphasis, including the words "legitimate self-defense." The Government of Israel is, of course, not bound by the domestic legislation of the United States. It is, nevertheless, bound by its acceptance of the substance of the statute through its agreement in its note of July 23, 1952 to the terms specified in the United States note of July 1, 1952. During the June, 1982 attack-invasion, as well as at other times, the United States Government has been, and is now, obligated to honor and enforce this "solemn international contract."[574] Because Israel was conducting a war which did not meet the legal requirements analyzed in Chapter II, Section B of (1) good faith use of peaceful procedures, (2) response to an actual or reasonably anticipated armed attack, and (3) proportionality in responding measures, it was conducting a war of aggression[575] and was in violation of the "legitimate self-defense" requirement of the Mutual Defense Assistance Agreement. It is unfortunate, but necessary, to conclude that the complete ignoring of or indifference to the Agreement demonstrated by Secretary Haig means that the United States participated with the State of Israel in violating it.[576]

Secretary Haig's treatment of a different international agreement provides an interesting comparison. It is well known that the United States diplomats who were unlawfully held as hostages by the Government of Iran were released as a result of the United States-Iranian Agreement effectuated at the end of President Carter's term of office. At a White House meeting, shortly after the release of the diplomats, the majority of President Reagan's advisers recommended that the Agreement be abrogated.[577] Haig understood the anger which was directed at the Iranian state terrorism. His clearly expressed conviction was that he was

---

571. The relevant Charter excerpts are set forth at the beginning of Chap. II.
572. Appendix D.
573. The technical consistency stated in the text does not lead to the conclusion that the Agreement is sound policy since continuing militarization is adverse to the legitimate interests of Israelis, Palestinians and others.
574. The words are Secretary Haig's but in reference to the U.S.-Iranian Agreement considered in the text accompanying *infra* note 580.
575. *Supra* note 571.
576. In the same way, Secretary Haig did nothing to prevent continual Israeli violation of the Israel-PLO Cease-Fire Agreement of July 24, 1981. Nor did he object to the persistent attempts to change the terms unilaterally by Prime Minister Begin. See, *e.g.* the text accompanying *supra* note 507.
577. Haig 78.

"appalled" that such a "cynical action" could be contemplated.[578] Although "deeply flawed" it was "a binding contract" in which the Carter Administration had pledged not only its word "but the honor of the United States Government."[579] His conclusion was that:

> No incoming Administration had the right to renounce lightly a solemn international contract entered into by its predecessor. We just couldn't do it.[580]

President Reagan was "nodding agreement" and the Agreement was honored.[581] In achieving this result, Secretary Haig was acting consistently with the basic international law doctrine of *pacta sunt servanda*—agreements will be observed. There is no reason to believe that the United States-Israel Mutual Defense Assistance Agreement is less subject to this basic doctrine. In fairness to Secretary Haig, this agreement was not "renounced" but was simply evaded.

The matters which have been considered above also involve possible criminal liability for officers of the United States Government if we may believe the considered legal opinion of Justice Robert Jackson set forth in Chapter II, Section C, that the standards applied to German defendants by the International Military Tribunal at Nuremberg (IMT) also apply to others.[582] The article of the Charter of the IMT concerning "Crimes Against Peace" has been considered.[583] It, and the other Nuremberg principles have been approved by the United Nations General Assembly and codified by the International Law Commission.[584] Principle VI in relevant part provides:

> The crimes hereinafter set out are punishable as crimes under international law:
>   a. Crimes against peace:
>   (i) Planning, preparation, initiation or waging of a war of aggression or a war in violation of international treaties, agreements or assurances;
>   (ii) Participation in a common plan or conspiracy for the accomplishment of any of the acts mentioned under (i).

In spite of the evidence presented so convincingly by Secretary Haig, there can be no determination of guilt without due process of law. The IMT was an *ad hoc* court and there is no contemporary international criminal court. Even though the evidence presented by Haig is sufficient to justify indictments, there still can be no judicial determination of innocence or guilt except by a properly constituted court and with the full opportunity for an adequate defense such as that which was afforded to German defendants.

---

578. *Id.*
579. *Id.*
580. *Id.*
581. *Id.* 78-79.
582. *Supra* note 165 and accompanying text.
583. The text accompanying *supra* notes 160-161.
584. G.A. Res. 177(II), *2 U.N. GAOR* 111-12 (21 Nov. 1947). The codification appears in, *inter alia,* 45 Am. J. Int'l L. Supp. 125 (1951). Principle III (*id.* at 128), like art. 7 of the Charter of the I.M.T. (1 I.M.T. 12) provides that the official status of an individual does not free him from criminal responsibility.

It would be an encouraging conclusion to the present chapter to be able to state that the United States Government's adherence to basic legal criteria improved upon the replacement of Secretary Haig. Unfortunately, the subsequent failure of the United States to implement its "guarantees" in the Agreement of August 19, 1982 concerning the protection of Palestinian civilians following the departure of the PLO combatants from Beirut, as well as other events, do not make such a conclusion possible.[585] The failure to implement the just-mentioned "guarantees" and the subsequent mass murders at Sabra and Shatila caused little or no official concern in the United States. The continuing double-standard of the U.S. Government may be amply illustrated by inquiring as to the degree of official concern which would exist if the victims of a similar attack were North American or European immigrants to Israel.

The central point to be emphasized is that the unlawful character of United States policy in the Middle East has not only been damaging to United States "prestige" and "credibility." It has also been a disaster to the legitimate national and humanitarian interests of Palestinians, Lebanese and Israelis, among others. Because of the demonstrated failure of policies based upon ignorance, prejudice, and perceived "power" or "strategic" considerations, a policy based upon law is no longer merely an idealistic alternative but it is the only practical alternative to the present course of continuing destruction of human and material values.[586]

Wide World Photos

Faces of this woman and her two children register the terror of the seige of West Beirut as they seized the opportunity of a cease fire August 2, 1982 to cross from the beseiged Western sector of the city into East Beirut.

---

585. The Agreement containing the United States "guarantees" is cited in *supra* note 396. The Agreement is considered in the note just cited and in *supra* notes 425-429 and accompanying text.
586. See *infra* note 601 and accompanying text.

V. Recommendations

The Israeli attack on the Palestinian people and invasion of Lebanon in the summer of 1982 involved major violations of the customary and treaty law which prohibits aggression and protects war victims. It is imperative that such violations not be condoned. An effective world legal order must, at the very least, provide protection from coercion and aggression,[587] and it is in the common interest of all to see that this legal order is reestablished.

It is important to recognize that Israel's invasion of Lebanon is integrally connected to its policy in the territories occupied in 1967. The destruction of the PLO which was a major motivation of the attack-invasion into Lebanon has been seen by then Defense Minister Sharon and others as being essential for Israel's implementation of its objectives in the West Bank and Gaza Strip. Mr. Sharon stated in June, 1982:

> The bigger the blow is and the more we damage the PLO infrastructure in Lebanon, the more the Arabs in the West Bank and Gaza will be ready to negotiate with us. . . . I am convinced that the echo of this campaign is reaching into the house of every Arab family in [the West Bank] and Gaza.[588]

Seen in this larger context, it is clear that the resolution of the conflict in Lebanon must be linked to a solution of the larger Palestine problem.

The application of sanctions to enforce the world community consensus concerning the conflict situation is indispensable. No organized community, domestic or international, can achieve even a minimum legal order without the ability and the will to use the necessary coercion to obtain it. The essential element is that coercion must be in the responsible hands of the community and not in the hands of a militaristic and expansionist state. The central point was made by Senator J.W. Fulbright some time ago when he wrote:

> The crucial distinction is not between coercion and voluntarism, but between duly constituted force applied through law. . .and the arbitrary coercion of the weak by the strong.[589]

The world community consensus concerning the invasion of Lebanon and the broader Palestine problem is probably best seen in the relevant United Nations resolutions concerning the area including Security Council resolution 242 which reflects the prohibition of the acquisition of territory by war.[590] It would be a most important step toward the settlement of the problem to enforce these resolutions through appropriate sanctions. When action by the Security Council is blocked by the negative vote of a permanent member, as it is in connection with sanctions against Israel, the Uniting for Peace Resolution[591] adopted during the Korean War is a precedent for such action to be taken by the General Assembly.

---

587. The world legal order is considered systematically in M.S. McDougal and Associates, *Studies in World Public Order* (1960).
588. Interview in *Time* magazine, June 21, 1982, p. 19.
589. *The Crippled Giant* 108 (Vintage Books, 1972).
590. *Supra* note 149.
591. G.A. Res. 377A (V), *5 U.N. GAOR, Supp. 20* (A/1775), pp. 10-12 (Nov. 3, 1950).

One of the objections that will be made to this recommendation for the application of adequate sanctions is that it is an "imposed settlement."[592] This objection should be clearly understood both in its explicit meaning and in its implication. Its explicit meaning is that an imposed settlement by the world community under law is opposed. Its unexpressed but necessary implication is that the existing settlement imposed by the military power of the Government of Israel is condoned. It is remarkable that this position applies only to the Israeli-Palestinian conflict. It overlooks the highly successful imposition of a settlement on Japan in the years following the end of the Second World War. It also fails to mention the imposed settlement in Europe at the end of the same war. One of the most successful imposed settlements in history was the peace which the Congress of Vienna imposed on France beginning in 1815.[593] The justice involved in that settlement, including the protection of legitimate French national interests, resulted in less coercion being required than would otherwise have been necessary. Both justice and coercion are typically required in peace settlements and where justice is used less, coercion must be used more.[594] The absence of elementary justice in the military settlement now imposed in the Middle East, including Palestine and Lebanon, leads to the great and increasing use of coercion.

Although sanctions which do not have the participation of the United States would not be sufficiently effective, it may be hoped that the combination of world community pressure and the increasing economic drain of support for Israel on the United States[595] will bring it back to the principled position taken by President Eisenhower when Israel refused to withdraw from Suez in response to the United Nations demand in 1957. President Eisenhower said:

> This raises a basic question of principle. Should a nation which attacks and occupies foreign territory in the face of United Nations disapproval be allowed to impose conditions on its own withdrawal?
>
> If we agree that armed attack can properly achieve the purpose of the assailant, then I fear we will have turned back the clock of international order. We will, in effect, have countenanced the use of force as a means of settling international differences and through this gaining national advantages.[596]
>
> * * *
>
> The United Nations must not fail. I believe that—in the interests of peace—the United Nations has no choice but to exert pressure upon Israel to comply with the withdrawal resolutions.[597]

Israel withdrew following the clear statement that the United States would support sanctions.

---

592. E.g., the opposition to such a settlement, as applied to Israel, expressed by Acting U.S. Ambassador to the United Nations, W.J. Vanden Heuvel, in the Emergency Special Session of the General Assembly on Palestine on July 24, 1980. 80 *U.S. Dept. State Bull.* 67 (Sept., 1980).

593. H.A. Kissinger, *A World Restored: Metternich, Castlereagh and the Problems of Peace, 1812-1822* (Sentry ed., undated).

594. S.P. Tillman, *The United States in the Middle East: Interests and Obstacles,* Chap. 7 entitled "Conclusions: On Peace and How to Get It" (1982).

595. Report of the Comptroller General of the United States, *U.S. Assistance to the State of Israel,* GAO/ID-83-51 (June 24, 1983) concludes that Israel will request substantial increases in the multi-billion dollar aid received from the United States unless there is an enduring peaceful settlement in the Middle East.

596. 36 *U.S. Dept. State Bull.* 387 at 389 (Mar. 11, 1957).

597. *Id.* at 390.

Because of the continuing Israeli economic crisis, largely caused by the militarization of its foreign policy and its domestic society, there is every reason to believe that economic sanctions would be successful in achieving Israeli compliance with the relevant United Nations resolutions.[598] Such sanctions would immediately raise a new hope in Israel on the part of those patriotic and enlightened Israeli citizens who have been urging their government to enter into a peaceful settlement. In the unlikely event that the economic sanctions were unsuccessful, military sanctions are available under the United Nations Charter. It is necessary to emphasize that sanctions must be conceptualized and applied as a comprehensive process, starting with persuasive measures and leading to increasingly coercive ones, rather than as a group of isolated and unrelated episodes.[599]

It is also imperative that the world community enforce the application of the customary and treaty humanitarian law. The state parties to the four Geneva Conventions of 1949 for the Protection of War Victims have agreed in the common article 1 to not only respect, but to "ensure respect" for the Conventions. Consequently, where one state party is in violation, the others are also in violation unless they take energetic measures to bring the violator into compliance. The grave breaches provisions of the Geneva Conventions and the precedent of the International Military Tribunal at Nuremberg provide existing legal authority for enforcement.[600]

The alternative to enforcement of the law is to accept an international system based upon the use of military power outside the law. Such a system is the antithesis of a just and stable peace and requires the entire world community to live under the cloud of impending nuclear catastrophe. In addition to removing this threat, the effective application of the relevant law in the Middle East will result in first the conservation and then the development of the human and material resources of all the peoples of the area through the achievement of peace based upon international law and the world legal order.[601]

---

598. *U.N. Charter* arts. 39-50 provide for sanctions.
599. The past performance and the present potential of such sanctions by the world community are analyzed in M.S. McDougal and F.P. Feliciano, *Law and Minimum World Public Order,* Chap. 4 entitled, "Community Sanctioning Process and Minimum Order" (1961).
600. See the text of Sec. III F *supra.*
601. The central point in the textual paragraph is persuasively developed and illustrated by examples in John A. Perkins, *The Prudent Peace: Law as Foreign Policy* (Univ. of Chicago, 1981).

    Following the terrorist attack on the U.S. Marine Barracks near the International Airport in Beirut, Secretary of Defense Weinberger appointed a distinguished commission of inquiry headed by Admiral Robert L.J. Long, USN (Ret.). It is significant that this commission made as one of its major recommendations "a more vigorous and demanding approach to pursuing diplomatic alternatives." *Report of the DOD Commission on Beirut International Airport Terrorist Act, October 23, 1983* pp. 122-23 (20 Dec. 1983).

APPENDIX A

Common Articles 1 and 2 of the Four Geneva Conventions of 1949 for the Protection of War Victims

Article 1. The High Contracting Parties undertake to respect and to ensure respect for the present Convention in all circumstances.

Art. 2. In addition to the provisions which shall be implemented in peace-time, the present Convention shall apply to all cases of declared war or of any other armed conflict which may arise between two or more of the High Contracting Parties, even if the state of war is not recognized by one of them.

The Convention shall also apply to all cases of partial or total occupation of the territory of a High Contracting Party, even if the said occupation meets with no armed resistance.

Although one of the Powers in conflict may not be a party to the present Convention, the Powers who are parties thereto shall remain bound by it in their mutual relations. They shall furthermore be bound by the Convention in relation to the said Power, if the latter accepts and applies the provisions thereof.

APPENDIX B

Article 4A of the Geneva Convention Relative to the Treatment of Prisoners of War (1949)

A. Prisoners of war, in the sense of the present Convention, are persons belonging to one of the following categories, who have fallen into the power of the enemy:

(1) Members of the armed forces of a Party to the conflict, as well as members of militias or volunteer corps forming part of such armed forces.

(2) Members of other militias and members of other volunteer corps, including those of organized resistance movements, belonging to a Party to the conflict and operating in or outside their own territory, even if this territory is occupied, provided that such militias or volunteer corps, including such organized resistance movements, fulfill the following conditions:

    (a) that of being commanded by a person responsible for his subordinates;

    (b) that of having a fixed distinctive sign recognizable at a distance;

    (c) that of carrying arms openly;

    (d) that of conducting their operations in accordance with the laws and customs of war.

(3) Members of regular armed forces who profess allegiance to a government or an authority not recognized by the Detaining Power.

(4) Persons who accompany the armed forces without actually being members thereof, such as civilian members of military aircraft crews, war correspondents, supply contractors, members of labour units or of services responsible for the welfare of the armed forces, provided that they have received authorization from the armed forces which they accompany, who shall provide them for that purpose with an identity card similar to the annexed model.

(5) Members of crews, including masters, pilots and apprentices, of the merchant marine and the crews of civil aircraft of the Parties to the conflict, who do not benefit by more favourable treatment under any other provisions of international law.

(6) Inhabitants of a non-occupied territory, who on the approach of the enemy spontaneously take up arms to resist the invading forces, without having had time to form themselves into regular armed units, provided they carry arms openly and respect the laws and customs of war.

APPENDIX C
Spanish Draft Resolution
U.N. Doc. S/15185

The Security Council,

Recalling its resolutions 508 (1982) and 509 (1982),

Taking note of the two positive replies to the Secretary-General of the Government of Lebanon and the Palestine Liberation Organization contained in document S/15178,

1. Condemns the non-compliance with resolutions 508 (1982) and 509 (1982) by Israel;

2. Urges the parties to comply strictly with the regulations attached to the Hague Convention of 1907;

3. Reiterates its demand that Israel withdraw all its military forces forthwith and unconditionally to the internationally recognized boundaries of Lebanon;

4. Reiterates also its demand that all parties observe strictly the terms of paragraph 1 of resolutions 508 (1982) which called on them to cease immediately and simultaneously all military activities within Lebanon and across the Lebanese-Israeli border;

5. Demands that within six hours all hostilities must be stopped in compliance with Security Council resolutions 508 (1982) and 509 (1982) and decides, in the event of non-compliance, to meet again to consider practical ways and means in accordance with the Charter of the United Nations.

APPENDIX D
95 U.S. Statutes at Large 1526

§ 2754. Purposes for which military sales or leases by United States are authorized; report to Congress

Defense articles and defense services shall be sold or leased by the United States Government under this chapter to friendly countries solely for internal security, for legitimate self-defense, to permit the recipient country to participate in regional or collective arrangements or measures consistent with the Charter of the United Nations, or otherwise to permit the recipient country to participate in collective measures requested by the United Nations for the purpose of maintaining or restoring international peace and security, or for the purpose of enabling foreign military forces in less developed friendly countries to construct public works and to engage in other activities helpful to the economic and social development of such friendly countries. It is the sense of the Congress that such foreign military forces should not be maintained or established solely for civic action activities and that such civic action activities not significantly detract from the capability of the military forces to perform their military missions and be coordinated with and form part of the total economic and social development effort: *Provided,* That none of the funds contained in this authorization shall be used to guarantee, or extend credit, or participate in an extension of credit in connection with any sale of sophisticated weapons systems, such as missile systems and jet aircraft for military purposes, to any underdeveloped country other than Greece, Turkey, Iran, Israel, the Republic of China, the Philippines and Korea unless the President determines that such financing is important to the national security of the United States and reports within thirty days each such determination to the Congress.

As amended Pub.L. 97-113, Title I, § 109(b)(3), Dec. 29, 1981, 95 Stat. 1526.

APPENDIX E

3 U.S. Treaties and Other International Agreements 4985

ISRAEL
MUTUAL DEFENSE ASSISTANCE

Agreement effected by exchange of notes signed at Tel Aviv July 1 and 23, 1952; entered into force July 23, 1952.

TIAS 2675
July 1, 23, 1952

The American Ambassador to the Israeli Acting Minister for Foreign Affairs

AMERICAN EMBASSY, TEL AVIV
July 1, 1952

No. 1

EXCELLENCY:

I have the honor to inform Your Excellency that the Government of Israel has been declared eligible to receive from the Government of the United States of America reimbursable military assistance under the provisions of Section 408(e) of the Mutual Defense Assistance Act of 1949 (Public Law 329, 81st Congress), as amended. The provisions of these laws and the policy of the United States Government require that certain assurances be received before completing any transactions under Section 408(e) of the Act.

63 Stat. 720.
22 U.S.C. § 1580.

It is the understanding of the United States Government that the Government of Israel is prepared to accept the following undertakings:

1. The Government of Israel agrees to use any assistance furnished under the Mutual Defense Assistance Act of 1949, as amended, to further the policies and purposes of that Act which are to foster international peace and security within the framework of the Charter of the United Nations through measures which will further the ability of nations dedicated to the principles and purposes of the Charter to participate effectively in arrangements for individual and collective self-defense in support of those purposes and principles. The Government of Israel further agrees to furnish equipment and materials, services, or other assistance, consistent with the Charter of the United Nations, to the United States or to and among other nations eligible for assistance under the Mutual Defense Assistance Act to further the policies and purposes of this Act, as set forth above, and as may be mutually agreed hereafter.

59 Stat. 1031.

2. The Government of Israel assures the United States Government that such equipment, materials, or services as may be acquired from the United States under the provisions of Section 408(c) of the Mutual Defense Assistance Act of 1949, as amended, are required for and will be used solely to maintain its internal security, its legitimate self-defense,

105

or to permit it to participate in the defense of the area of which it is a part, or in United Nations collective security arrangements and measures, and that it will not undertake any act of aggression against any other state.

3. The Government of Israel will not relinquish title to or possession of any equipment and materials, information or services furnished under Section 408(e) of the Mutual Defense Assistance Act of 1949, as amended, without the consent of the United States Government.

4. The Government of Israel will protect the security of any article, service or information furnished under Section 408(e) of the Mutual Defense Assistance Act of 1949, as amended.

5. The Government of Israel understands that, prior to the transfer of any item or the rendering of any services, the United States Government retains the right to terminate the transaction.

6. The Government of Israel is prepared to accept terms and conditions of payment for any item or service which may be furnished under the Mutual Defense Assistance Act of 1949, as amended, which are in accord with the provisions of Section 408(e)(2) of this Act.

I have the honor to propose that this note, together with your reply confirming these assurances, constitute an agreement between the Government of the United States of America and the Government of Israel, effective on the date of your Note.

Accept, Excellency, the renewed assurances of my highest consideration.

MONNETT B. DAVIS

His Excellency
DAVID BEN GURION,
Acting Minister for Foreign Affairs,
Hakirya.

The Israeli Minister for Foreign Affairs
to the American Ambassador

MINISTRY FOR FOREIGN AFFAIRS
HAKIRYA, ISRAEL
23rd July 1952

Sir:

I have the honor to refer to your note of July 1, 1952, concerning certain assurances and undertakings required from the Israel Government prior to the completion of transactions between the Israel Government and the United States Government under the provisions of Section 408(e) of the Mutual Defense Assistance Act of 1949, as amended.

The Government of Israel accepts the undertakings and assurances outlined in that note and concurs with proposal that this note, together with your note dated July 1, 1952, referred to above, constitute an agreement covering all transactions for the supply of military assistance under Section 408(e) of the Mutual Defense Assistance Act of 1949, as amended, between the respective governments, the said agreement to enter into force on the date of this note.

I avail myself of this opportunity to renew to you the assurances of my highest consideration.

M. SHARETT

The Honorable
MONNETT B. DAVIS,
Ambassador of the United States of America,
Tel Aviv.

Index to Legal Sources

Publications About the Middle East from
the American Educational Trust

White Papers

Publications in the American Educational Trust "White Paper" series dealing with Middle Eastern political affairs are available at $1.00 each including postage, or at 60 cents each for bulk orders of 10 or more copies of each title. Titles include:

MAPS AND MYTHOLOGY—What Israeli Records Reveal About the Land and People of Palestine .... By Edward F. Henderson

DEFENSE OR AGGRESSION—U.S. Arms Export Control Laws and the Israeli Invasion of Lebanon .... By William Espinosa and Les Janka

SETTLEMENTS AND THE LAW—A Juridical Analysis of the Israeli Settlements in the Occupied Territories .... By Sally V. Mallison and W. Thomas Mallison

POLES AND PALESTINIANS—Labouring Under Oppression .... By Paul Harper

KEYS TO CONTROL—Israel's Pursuit of Arab Water Resources .... By Leslie Schmida

American Educational Trust Books

A CHANGING IMAGE—American Perceptions of the Arab-Israeli Dispute 1945-1985 ......By Richard H. Curtiss......$12.95 including postage ($7.75 each for bulk order of 10 or more copies)

THE ARABS 1984-85: Atlas and Almanac ....By John C. Kimball..................$7.95 including postage (orders of 10 or more $4.80 each)

SUBSCRIPTION SERVICES

The Washington Report on Middle East Affairs

This twelve-page newsletter is published 16 times per year and offers in-depth analysis of Middle East political and economic developments of concern to the United States. Subscriptions are $50 for institutions; $25 for individuals and educational institutions ($25 for each additional subscription sent to the same mailing address); $50 for overseas subscribers. Introductory copies are mailed at no charge.

Middle East Clipboard

This weekly clipping service provides significant English-language press and periodical coverage of the Middle East, the Islamic countries, and U.S. relations with those countries. It averages 150 pages per week. Clippings are photocopied on 8 × 10 white paper and indexed for permanent filing. Subscribers receive an annual index at no extra charge. Cost is $365 per year in the U.S. Introductory service is mailed at no charge.